SALLUST

The Conspiracy of Catiline
And
The War of Jugurtha

A New Translation
With Notes, Commentary, and Illustrations

By
QUINTUS CURTIUS

SALLUST:
The Conspiracy of Catiline and The War of Jugurtha

Cover design by James Seehafer

Printed in Charleston, South Carolina

Published by Fortress of the Mind Publications™
www.qcurtius.com

ISBN-13: 978-0-578-43124-6

An obscure prophecy is appropriate for the diviners and oracles of the gods; but someone who wants certainty goes away wiser if he seeks the truth from the relics of the dead and the oracles of harsh fate.

Lucan, *Pharsalia* VI.770

TABLE OF CONTENTS

SALLUST

The Conspiracy of Catiline
And
The War of Jugurtha

I. FOREWORD

My first encounter with Sallust came many years ago when I was a student. He is not a writer easily forgotten. Not only was he able to tell an exciting story, but he could do it in a way that elevated events from their immediate temporal environs to a place where he could convey the profoundest lessons about character, fate, and the dangers of hubris. His writing was swift, compact, and rhetorically luminous. Who today would dare to begin a historical work with the sublime invocation that opens the *Conspiracy of Catiline*?

All men who seek to be better than the animals ought to exert themselves with the greatest efforts, lest they pass their lives in silence as if they were beasts of burden, which Nature has conditioned to be prostrate and subservient to their stomachs. All our powers are situated in our minds and bodies; we make use of the mind more for control, and the body for service. One of these we hold in common with the gods, and the other with the wild beasts. For me it seems more proper to seek glory through one's natural character than through the efforts of naked force and, since this life that we delight in is short, to fashion a legacy for ourselves that is as lasting as possible. For glory derived from riches and appearances is transitory and brittle, but masculine virtue is pure and eternal.[1]

---

[1] *Catiline* I.

This is a historian with an unapologetic conception of man and his place in the natural order of things, a historian who has seen and done much and who now intends to pass on what he has learned. No less impressive are the stirring opening sentences of *The War of Jugurtha*:

In vain does man lament his nature over the fact that it is fragile and impermanent and governed more by chance than by virtue. Deeper inquiry shows, however, that you will find nothing greater or more surpassing, and that human nature more often lacks perseverance than physical strength or an extended age. But the mind is the leader and commander of the life of mortals. He who marches to glory by the path of virtue has an abundance of strength, power, and renown; he does not need fortune, since fortune can neither bestow nor revoke from someone honesty, industry, or any of the other noble qualities. The man consumed by perverse appetites surrenders himself to inertia and the basest cravings of the body. For a short time he enjoys his destructive lusts, where strength, opportunity, and good character are drained away through self-indulgence. Blame is fixed on the "infirmity of human nature," and the engineers of the crime transfer responsibility to some external factor. But if men had the same care for doing good works as they have enthusiasm for chasing what is of no advantage to them—in many cases what is even dangerous and harmful to them—they would more often *rule* fortune than *be ruled* by it, and would advance to such greatness that through their glory they would become immortal among men.[2]

---

[2] *Jugurtha* I.

With Sallust's works there was no padding or "filler": every word and every sentence counted. Like most of the great Roman writers, he believed that fate (*fortuna*) had the final say in the outcome of human affairs, but that a man's bearing or manly virtue (*virtus*) could tip the scales in his favor at critical moments. There was a majestic, inspiring quality to his prose; its brevity (and occasional obscurity) seemed to challenge the reader to draw his own inferences and conclusions from the events related. Sallust never condescends to his audience. Unlike some of his Greek predecessors, he has no desire to spoon-feed readers with fables, legends, or details that should be clear from context. This is a hard-headed, practical man of experience and substance, a man who expects his fellow travelers to employ basic deductive skills.

Many years passed after that first encounter with the historian. I happened to find him again at another point in my life, a time when I was leaving the military and embarking on a civilian career. It was a time of transition and turbulence, and one not without uncertainty. A second reading of the historian revealed new perspectives, lessons, and insights that had not been apparent to me before. Perhaps it is true, as the French writer François-René de Chateaubriand said, that we are not just one person in our lives; we are instead a composite of different "lives" laid end to end as one phase of life dissolves into the next. We are different people with a separate consciousness at each one of these phases. Reading Sallust a second time, I was especially struck by the power of Marius's speech to the commons.[3] The oration that Sallust gives him ranks as one of the most scorching indictments of unearned privilege ever written. Marius's words sailed like an arrow to my heart: I felt as if he were speaking directly to me.

Yet careful readings of the original text convinced me that the existing translations of Sallust did not give many passages the full

---

[3] Jug. LXXXIV-LXXXV.

resonance in English that they deserved. This was especially true in the *Jugurtha*, where the relationship between the commanders Marius and Metellus, the descriptions of some of the battles, and the explanations of certain tactical and administrative matters would greatly benefit from a translator with practical military experience. There were other deficiencies that needed to be addressed as well. Until now no translator has called sufficient attention to the counterinsurgency aspects of the *Jugurtha*. Its modern relevance has never been more obvious. The inclusion of chronological tables, maps, and diagrams could assist the reader who had little or no experience in Roman military or political history. It was then that my desire to translate Sallust was born. What I felt was needed was a fully modern translation that provided the reader with essential details—in one place—to enhance understanding and enjoyment of the text.

Sallust was the first of the great Roman historians and his influence has been considerable. He was studied by the rhetoricians (e.g. Quintilian) and imitated by those who came after him (e.g., Tacitus). Like any great man he had more than his share of detractors; but it cannot be disputed that his works have been taught and studied for many centuries. In the nineteenth and early twentieth centuries of our own era, numerous "school editions" of his works were used as college texts for advanced students of Latin. Sadly, with the general decline in classical studies since the mid-twentieth century, the pleasures of reading him have been denied several generations of students. What the reader of 2017 needs is a new translation—annotated and illustrated—that presupposes no knowledge of Roman history and is not burdened by old-fashioned English stylistics. This was the approach taken in my translation of Cicero's *On Duties* and I have found that it has resonated positively with readers.

This translation of Sallust is designed for the general reader who wishes to have an edition that is entirely self-contained. Specific tools are included in this volume to assist in comprehension. There are notes, maps, illustrations, a detailed introduction, chronological tables, an index, and topical charts. Every effort has been made to ensure that the reader is given the necessary tools to understand and enjoy these two great historical monographs.

A translation of this kind is a creative literary endeavor in its own right. Sallust's prose presents challenges that are not found in Cicero or any other Latin writer. Where Cicero is effusive and lengthy, Sallust is dense, compact, sententiously brief, and elusive; sometimes what he does *not* say matters as much as what he does say. He was fond of dropping elliptical hints and expecting his readers to supply their own conclusions. He has a preference for archaic constructions in Latin, unusual words and spellings, and highly rhetorical grammatical forms. At his best he reads like a prose poet, balancing out his clauses as if he were counting syllables in classical verse. But the overall effect is powerful and unforgettable. A translator cannot take too many liberties with his words; this would dilute the force of his diction and compromise his literary techniques.

I am indebted to the many people who assisted in the preparation of this book. The artist James Seehafer, who produced the wonderful cover for *On Duties* in 2016, came through once again with cover art that does justice to Sallust's timeless themes. As always, Zeljko Ivic offered consistent encouragement at every step of the journey. Ole Brandenburg provided invaluable assistance with the mapping software used in the text. My father patiently proofread the entire manuscript, offering many editing suggestions that I would otherwise have missed. Finally, I must thank the many readers whose private emails and expressions of support were both a stimulus and a solace. May they never be silent.

Quintus Curtius
May 2017

II. INTRODUCTION

A. THE LIFE OF SALLUST

Caius Sallustius Crispus was born in 86 B.C. at the Sabine town of Amiternum.[4] His family seems to have been of modest means, and he was able to receive a decent education in Rome. We know very little about his early life; but his non-aristocratic origins may provide a clue in explaining the historian's seething antagonism towards the nobility. Judging from the accusations of moral looseness made against him by his political enemies, we may guess that he enjoyed himself as a youth. He obtained the quaestorship and a senate seat in 59 B.C. Seven years later he was a tribune of the plebs. By this time he was fully embroiled in the turbulent—and brutal—factional politics of his era. He was involved in prosecuting Milo, the assassin of the popularist politician Publius Clodius Pulcher; this set him against the powerful Cicero, who was defending Milo. The end result of his forays into politics was that Sallust was expelled from the senate in 50 B.C. for alleged moral turpitude.

This must have stoked the fires of his already strong anti-patrician sentiments. His own words about his early experiences in senatorial politics are revealing:

Like many others, I was led as a young man by my formative interests into the world of public affairs, and there

---

[4] Amiternum is located northeast of Rome in the Abruzzo region, near the city of L'Aquila.

found many things arrayed against me. Recklessness, bribery, and greed flourished at the expense of modesty, self-control and virtue. Although a proud soul rejects these sorts of evil practices, in the presence of so much vice my tender age was gripped by corrupt ambition. And although I dissented from the wayward behavior of others, still my longing for rewards harassed me with their same unwelcome notoriety and jealousy.[5]

One detects in the above passage a hint of guilt at recalling some activities of his early manhood. The writer Aulus Gellius relates an anecdote that Sallust was whipped and fined for a sexual indiscretion;[6] but Gellius was a nobleman writing 150 years after the fact. Sallust was living in a corrupt age; if he occasionally crossed moral lines, it is doubtful that he was much worse than most of his contemporaries. More likely is the explanation that his lack of aristocratic contacts left him no safety net when factional fighting generated casualties. He was probably also known by this time as a follower of Julius Caesar, Rome's greatest maverick and rebel. Sallust's senatorial colleagues, aristocrats who feared and disliked Caesar, almost certainly seized on an expedient pretext to deprive him of his seat. In Sallust's day the political landscape of Rome was divided into two major factions: the *populares* (popular party) and the *optimates* (aristocrats). Sallust had cast his lot with the popular party and with Julius Caesar; although Caesar was an aristocrat, he knew Rome needed to build a more inclusive political system and remained a dissenter from the prejudices common to his class.

His star rose with Caesar's. In 47 B.C.—after the Battle of Pharsalia, the event that clinched Caesar's victory in the civil war—Sallust was able to return to the senate as a praetor. From

---

[5] *Cat.* III.
[6] *Attic Nights* XVII.18.

this point his loyal service to Caesar continued to the very end. He went with him to Africa in 46 B.C. to mop up the remnants of Pompey's forces. Sallust remained there as governor of Numidia when Caesar left. For the great man to trust the young Sallust with such responsibility says much about the historian's qualities of character; Caesar was a keen judge of men and not given to sentimental appointments where real power was concerned. Nevertheless, Sallust's time in Numidia was marred by controversy. He is said to have engaged in corruption and extortion. When he returned to Rome about 45 B.C., formal charges were filed against him; the intervention of his patron Caesar apparently saved him from conviction. Some accounts have Sallust actually giving Caesar a share of his spoils in return for prosecutorial immunity. What are we to make of these stories?

We must remember that the time Sallust was living in was one of civil war, economic turbulence, and bitter factionalism. It was a standard feature of political life for public figures to hurl the most venomous accusations against each other; one has only to read the speeches of the day to see just how vituperative Roman politicians could be to each other. We must also be mindful of the fact that Caesar, like all great men, inspired both deep loyalty and bitter hatred. The nobles despised him for his progressive policies, egalitarian spirit, and his popularity with the masses. Sallust, as one of Caesar's inner circle, would have come under this same cloud of sentiment; and it was the aristocrats—not the commoners—who wrote the history books that have come down to us.

It is quite possible that while in Numidia he was acting under Caesar's orders, and that his financial squeezing of the province was done with his patron's full knowledge and approval. Caesar always needed money to fund his ambitious projects, and he could be as ruthless as anyone to achieve his objectives. Perhaps it was not Caesar who protected Sallust, but the other way around. Sallust may have been told (or implicitly encouraged) to squeeze the province for money on Caesar's behalf, and was then obligated to take the blame for his boss, who quietly had the charges against his deputy annulled. These are speculations, of course, but reasonable speculations nonetheless. The lack of available information means that the full details may never be known.

In any case, Sallust believed the time had come to retire from public life around 44 B.C. He may have been forced to do so by Caesar's assassination. He bought a villa at Tibur and constructed a beautiful aggregation of gardens in the Roman suburbs that came to be called the *Horti Sallustiani*. These gardens were so sumptuous that they even became retreats for future emperors. From this point in his life Sallust devoted his time to literary pursuits, writing the historical works that secured his reputation. Perhaps because of his loyal service to Caesar, he was untouched by the purges and chaos that gripped Rome in the wake of Caesar's assassination. (Yet another clue that he was known to have taken the blame for following orders.) He died in 34 B.C. at the age of fifty-two. Sallust must have been well-liked by his contemporaries and posterity, for his house was preserved and remained standing in Rome centuries later. The Greek historian Procopius notes that Sallust's house was burned by Alaric's troops when the Visigoths attacked Rome in 410 A.D.[7]

B. THE STYLE

Sallust's unique and idiosyncratic style has been the subject of commentary for centuries. Students of Latin well know his peculiarities: his preference for antique spellings, words, and phrases; his use of the so-called "historical infinitive" verbal form; the compact brevity of the narrative; and his fondness for

---

[7] *History of the Wars* III.2.24.

alliteration and antithesis in sentence structure. Not all of these stylistic features can be reproduced in English. But it is possible to come close. As noted above, Sallust disdained "padding" or "filler" in his writings. Every sentence, every clause, had a purpose. He does not waste time giving too much background information in his narratives. The rudimentary ethnographic information he gives about North Africa in *Jugurtha* (XVII—XIX) is only as long as it has to be, and no more. He does not fulminate against or denounce the characters in his histories; he lays out his own value system, describes the actions of the principals, and expects his readers to draw their own conclusions from what they read.

What remain are historical accounts of stark but surpassing beauty. Among the many unforgettable passages in Sallust, the following stand out: the indictment of Roman corruption in *Cat.* XXXVI *et. seq.*; the fearsome description of the blood-soaked battlefield in *Jug.* CI; the fighting death of Catiline and the lamentation of the survivors in *Cat.* LXI; the post-victory celebrations in *Jug.* LIII; the brilliant speeches of Caesar, Cato, and Marius; the gyrating spectators of the cavalry battle in *Jug.* LX; the savage slaughter of the trapped Roman garrison at Vaga in *Jug.* LXVII; the dramatic fall of Capsa and its terrifying aftermath in *Jug.* XCI; and the strange legend of the Philaeni brothers in *Jug.* LXXIX. Once read, these passages are never forgotten.

C. THE HISTORICAL WORKS

The surviving completed works of Sallust are contained in this volume. These works are the two monographs *The Conspiracy of Catiline* and *The War of Jugurtha*. Sallust also wrote an extensive history of his own times known as the *Histories*, but this survives only in pitiful fragments. The *Histories* was intended to cover in five books the twelve-year period from 78 to 67 B.C., and it is a great tragedy that it has not come down to us intact. Its few coherent passages (four speeches and a few letters, along with bits and pieces quoted by other authors) are very impressive, and would have told us much about a crucial period of the late Roman republic.

The *Conspiracy of Catiline* was composed before the *Jugurtha*. The surviving manuscripts give it several different titles; we do not know what Sallust's own preference was. The work describes an attempted takeover of the Roman government by a renegade nobleman named Lucius Catiline. While we cannot be certain of the year of its composition, a date sometime between 44 and 40 B.C. is probably correct. It is likely that the work was intended for a popular audience that would have hungered for a racy, lurid account of the events leading up to the attempted coup d'état. But like every great historian, Sallust manages to take a relatively minor episode and elevate it to supreme moral significance. *Catiline* manages to be both an exciting drama and a supremely relevant study of the pathology of moral corruption.

Although some of the chronology in the story is imprecise, Sallust made scrupulous use of the sources available to him, such as the senatorial archives and personal interviews. The speeches he puts in the mouths of Julius Caesar and Cato are both masterpieces of political oratory and revealing expositions of different philosophies. The character profiles of the other figures in the drama are vividly drawn and linger in the memory long after the narrative has ended. Sallust explains (*Cat.* IV) that his reasons for choosing to write an account of the conspiracy had to do with the "uniqueness" of the crime and the peril to which the republic was exposed. Some scholars, however, have suspected that a secondary motive may have been to clear his patron Caesar of any involvement in the affair.

The War of Jugurtha (*Bellum Jugurthinum*) is a longer, more complex, and richly layered work. It was probably composed in

41 B.C., but Sallust must have begun collecting source material for the book during his time in Numidia. He tells us (*Jug.* XVII) that he even had Punic books translated for him during the course of his research. The work describes the origin and conduct of Rome's counter-insurgency war against the wily Numidian king Jugurtha. Even when describing foreign wars, Sallust could not fail to register his antipathy to the Roman nobility. He tells us that he chose the Jugurthine war as his subject because of the war's "changeable fortunes" and because it was the beginning of the successful fight against the power of the nobility (*Jug.* V). Rome always looked on Africa with a bit of nervousness since the defeat of Carthage in the Third Punic War (149—146 B.C.). They saw it as their backyard and were careful to monitor events there. The trauma of a previous experience with an African adventurer (Hannibal) made Rome wary of the designs of Jugurtha, who carried all the warning signs of being an adventurer who would upset Roman colonial designs in Africa.

D. SALLUST AS A HISTORIAN

Sallust is the first Roman historian whose work has come down to us in complete form. He was a trailblazer of Latin historiography who had to cut a path through thickets that no predecessor had entered. Before him in Latin there were only chroniclers, not proper historians; for his model Sallust therefore looked to the towering influence of the fifth-century Greek historian Thucydides. The similarities between the two are more than just literary. Like Sallust, Thucydides also had frustrating experiences with politics. During the Peloponnesian War in 423 B.C., Thucydides as a general had been wrongly blamed for the fall of the city of Amphipolis, when he could not reach it in time to prevent it from coming under Spartan control. For this he was banished from Athens. This bitter experience permanently colored his view of politics and helped give him that detached and coldly analytical approach to human affairs. Sallust, as we have seen, also fared rather badly in these same arenas. But just as in the case of the Renaissance political theorist Machiavelli many centuries later, failure seemed actually to help Sallust as a historian. He had no illusions about the motivations of men and the realities of power: painful experience had acutely sharpened his powers of observation, giving his prose an immediate and incisive quality.

Sallust was highly regarded in antiquity. Seneca the Elder thought him superior to Thucydides in his mastery of the epigrammatic style;[8] the rhetorician Quintilian considered him a better historian than Livy.[9] Like any great man, he had his critics. Suetonius counseled students against imitating Sallust's "obscurity" and "bold verbal imagery;"[10] but this was more out of deference to a stylistic master than anything else. Only Sallust, he knew, could or should write like Sallust. The moral tone of his works triggered the antagonism of Macrobius (writing four hundred years after Sallust's death), who called Sallust *gravissimus alienae luxuriae obiurgator et censor* ("a very harsh judge and critic of the others' pleasures").[11] But this is unfair. If Sallust talked much about virtue, fortitude, and moral rectitude, it was because his life experiences had seared the importance of these things in his brain.

He lived through a period when the Roman republic had been ripped apart by the factionalism, selfishness, and greed of the nobility. This was what drew him instinctively to Julius Caesar, the reformer and maverick; we cannot understand Sallust unless we appreciate this basic truth. Like Machiavelli, Sallust was at the

---

[8] *Controversiae* IX.1
[9] *Inst. Ora.* II.5.19; see also X.1.101.
[10] *Gramm.* X.7.
[11] *Saturnalia* III.13.9.

same time both a practical realist and an idealist. He wanted to restore the values and ethos of the old republic as an antidote to the pervasive evils he saw around him. He may also have been tormented by feelings of guilt about the frivolities of his youth. But even if this is true, it hardly makes his views less valid. One could argue that Sallust's supposedly wild youth actually made him *more* credible as a moralist: no one takes seriously moral counsel proffered by a goody two shoes.

What are the basic tenets of his philosophy? Three Sallustian motifs appear repeatedly in his works: moral corruption, fortune, and virtue. He is obsessed with the moral decay brought on by excessive wealth. As the prologue to *Catiline* makes very clear (X-XIII), Sallust believed that the expanding Roman empire's military acquisitions had set in motion a process of moral corruption and political decay. But this process of decay could be reversed by implementing the mores and virtues of "our ancestors" (*mos maiorum*). While fortune seems to have the final say in human affairs (*Cat.* VIII), it can still be very much influenced by a man's virtue (*virtus*). *Virtus* for Sallust meant manliness, valor, or strength of character. For Sallust, an adverse change in fortune is usually the result of degenerate behavior caused by corrupted morals.[12] If so, then the reverse was also true: a man could turn fortune to his favor by exercising his masculine virtue. His anger and sorrow at the failure of his countrymen to preserve the character and moral qualities of their ancestors are expressed in the opening chapters of *Jugurtha* (I—IV). For Sallust, character is everything. Without it, a man is of no consequence; he will forever remain a useful pawn in the service of the rich and powerful.

---

[12] The humanist Francesco Petrarca was deeply impressed by this observation of Sallust. He devoted a good deal of space to it in a letter to Peter of Poitou in 1361. *See* Fantham, E., *Francesco Petrarca: Selected Letters* (Vol. I), Cambridge: Harvard Univ. Press, 2017, p. 523.

Thus masculine virtue has the power to influence fortune and avert the trajectory of fate. Sallust makes this clear in *Jugurtha* when he relates how Metellus whipped his demoralized, corrupted soldiers into fighting shape (*Jug.* XLIV). Metellus's predecessor in command in Numidia had allowed morale and discipline in the legions to become dangerously lax. As soon as he arrived on the scene, Metellus made bold changes. He got rid of camp followers and personal servants; he made every man carry his own arms and food; and he instilled a vigorous regime of marching, drilling, and camp construction. Only someone who has been in military environments in the field can understand how effective these types of measures can be. As far as Sallust is concerned, this restoration of virtue and banishment of corruption was the major reason for the military victories over Jugurtha that followed.

A man's fortune is to a large degree in his own hands: he himself—and not blind fate—must decide whether to adopt the path of virtue. Sallust knew the hearts of men, and he had learned his lessons the hard way. It would be too much to call him a cynic, but he has no illusions about altruism in politics and war. Commenting wryly on the celebrations of the Romans after a battle (*Jug.* LIII), he notes, "The ecstatic soldiers yelled out to each other and chattered about what they had done and heard; each man embellished his own deeds to the heavens. Human affairs naturally have this quality: the craven may boast in times of victory, but failure vilifies even the valiant." One senses Sallust is hinting that bad things are waiting for his countrymen right around the corner.

We have noted above that Sallust's consistent themes are moral corruption, virtue, and the variability fortune. These different strands are woven together in his writings in the service of two very old ideas that dated back to the ancient Greek tragedians. The ideas are (1) character determines fate; and (2) an excess of hubris and ambition inevitably leads a man to ruin. Sallust took these concepts very seriously and attributes the ruin of both Catiline and Jugurtha to their failure to restrain their ambitions. He credits them both with being men of great intelligence, ability, personal charm, and charisma. But since something was not in proper alignment in their characters, they allowed their flaws to consume any good qualities they may have had.

Catiline, for example, Sallust portrays as a charismatic leader who might have devoted himself to the service of the state. To make this point, he deliberately contrasts Catiline with Cicero and allows the reader to draw his own conclusions. Yet Catiline was also arrogant, ambitious, and entirely amoral; and these traits proved to be his undoing. Even so, Sallust is reasonably fair to him; he acknowledges his physical bravery in battle and describes his last stand with poignancy (*Cat.* LX). The same technique is used with Jugurtha. He is described as an intelligent, brave, and charismatic leader who greatly distinguished himself early in life; yet his paranoia and ambition proved to be uncontrollable. He turned on his relatives, attempted to seize sole power for himself in Numidia, and piloted a collision course with the Romans. Sallust's portrayal of Jugurtha is never one-dimensional; he is simultaneously presented as a villainous renegade, an object of sympathy (due to his lowly origins), and as a "nationalist" leader resisting Rome's invasion army. While each reader must decide for himself Jugurtha's ultimate significance, Sallust makes it clear that it was hubris that brought him from the dizzying heights of power in Numidia to being paraded in chains before the Roman populace.

These timeless themes and lessons are what make Sallust so relevant to us today. He reminds us that ability, brilliance, and ambition are ultimately useless unless tempered by character, discipline, and restraint. Fortune will always be changeable, twisting now one way, and now another. But the constancy of a man's character can stabilize his ship on the rolling sea of life, give him the means to weather the storms of fate, and permit him finally to turn fortune to his advantage.

E. POLITICAL AND MILITARY ORGANIZATION OF THE REPUBLIC

Perhaps Rome's greatest gift to the Western world was her mastery of the art of government. It would not be an exaggeration to say that no other people has equaled her in this respect. To get the most out of reading Sallust, it is important to understand the basics of how the Romans governed themselves during the republican period. During Rome's long existence as a cohesive nation, its system of government changed significantly: it was first a kingdom, then a republic, and then an imperial system. We will here discuss the republican system.[13]

To understand the Roman republican system, we must see it as the outcome of the interaction between the different "branches" of government: magistrates, popular assemblies, the senate, and (to a much lesser extent) religious structures. It was not a democracy; power firmly resided in the hands of the aristocracy (as in most societies then and now), but there were admirable checks and balances that allowed the different social classes to have a voice. At the top of the totem pole were the patricians (*patricii* or aristocrats); below them were the *equites* or "knights" (businessmen); and below these were the plebians (the common people). Slaves, if they mattered at all, were at the very bottom of the hierarchy. There was some mobility between the classes, but not much. The hierarchy was based more on birth and background than wealth; some plebians and *equites* were able to amass considerable wealth.

We will begin with the magistracies. These were various civil offices that also had some involvement in military affairs:

Praetor. This was a judicial official who ran the courts and issued legal decisions in the form of praetorian edicts. At times he

---

[13] "Republic" literally meant "the people's property" or "public thing" (*res publica*). *See* Cicero *De re publica* I.25.

could even command military units. There were normally eight praetors, and they were of two types: the *praetor urbanus* (responsible for Roman municipal affairs) and the *praetor peregrinus* (dealing with disputes between non-Romans). A man had to be at least thirty-nine to be elected praetor, and they were elected by an assembly called the *comitia centuriata*. Being a praetor was an important position; they could stand-in for the consul when he was away from Rome or on a military campaign. The praetor's power (*imperium*) was represented by six lictors (civil servants who acted as bodyguards).

Quaestor. The origin of this title is from the verb *quaerere* (to ask or seek). Quaestors handled financial matters, treasury issues, and governmental records. Like the praetors, during times of war they could find themselves commanding units in the field under the supervision of a consul. There were about twenty quaestors, and a man had to be at least thirty to be chosen for the office.

Aedile. This was a municipal government office responsible for public works and infrastructure. Roads, bridges, buildings, the public granary, and related issues came under the control of the aedile. It was also customary for the aedile to keep the populace entertained with games, festivals, gladiatorial combats, and other amusements. Not unsurprisingly, the office was used as a kind of political stepping stone to get one's name in the public mind.

Censor. Censors, of course, handled the five-year Roman census. The censor was not just a head-counter; he also functioned as a modern tax-assessor and an awarder of government contracts. Every man had his wealth and property surveyed; the idea was to find out who had what. One interesting part of the job of censor was that he acted as a guardian of public morals; censors had the power to issue invasive rules designed to curb extravagance. Such "sumptuary laws" were usually as ineffective then as they have been in modern times; but censors could remove a senator from office for moral indecency.

Consul. At the top of the civil office pyramid was the consul. There were two of them, and each could check the power of the other.

They were chosen every year from among the distinguished candidates who were expected already to have served in a lesser office. To be chosen consul was the highest political honor a man could attain, and it granted that man's family enduring notoriety. Roman historians often dated events by naming the consuls in office during the events, in the same way the Greek historians counted by Olympiads. This tradition has been respected in the chronological tables in this book. Consuls were attended by twelve lictors carrying the symbolic bundles of rods with an axe called *fasces*. Consuls led armies in battle and had nearly absolute power over their men in the field; they could also propose laws and negotiate treaties. Although their fame was great, their office was a short one (only a year). A man had to be at least forty-two to be consul. In practice, the office usually went to a man of patrician background, but there were occasional exceptions (Cicero being one).

Dictator. In theory the senate (or the consuls) could recommend a dictator be appointed in times of extreme national crisis. In practice this was not a common event; the crisis had to be extreme. One was chosen, for example, during Hannibal's invasion of Italy in the Second Punic War. Because of the traditional Roman distrust of absolute power, the office of dictator was only six months in duration. But during this time, his power was nearly absolute.

The Romans valued a background in public service and strong character as prerequisites for office. A man seeking office was first expected to have military experience with the legions; it was seen as the first crucible of character development. After this, he might run for the offices of quaestor or aedile and get his name known to the public. Candidates had to wait for three years between leaving the office of praetor and running for consul. This "path of honors" (*cursus honorum*) ensured that only men of proven worth and tested experience—and not frauds or demagogues—attained the highest offices.

The **Roman senate** was not exactly a legislative body in the modern sense. It did not actually pass laws; it was an advisory body consisting of aristocrats who had served as consuls, quaestors, praetors, censors, and tribunes. It thus carried tremendous prestige and its opinion could never be ignored by a consul who expected to stay in good graces. The senate (which met in the Curia) did have authority over revenues and expenses as well as issues related to the governance of the provinces. The senate was also fond of arbitrating disputes between political opponents and even foreign kings. Senators were not elected and they received no salary; once appointed, they retained their seats for life unless they might be removed for bad behavior. Although in theory there were rules preventing conflicts of interest, some senators found ways to profit directly or indirectly from their positions.

The interests of the plebians were represented by the **popular assemblies** (*comitia*). The *consilium plebis* (popular assembly) elected popular tribunes (*tribunus*). Since they had such large constituencies, the popular tribunes wielded great power in practice. The popular assembly could pass laws even without senatorial approval. There was another popular assembly called the *comitia centuriata* that elected the various magistrates, debated laws proposed by the senate, and performed other legislative functions.

Even religion was harnessed to the service of the state. A body of priests (*pontifices*) supervised the religious needs of the people; the head priest was called the *pontifex maximus*. They did not have legislative or administrative powers but they did act as advisors to political figures. As they did have influence over the popular mind through religious figures like augurs (who sought to interpret the will of the gods), they could never be completely ignored by a prudent political figure.

This complicated system of government, with its elaborate checks and balances, was stable and durable.[14] It also placed a

---

[14] Its influence persists down to the present day. The founders of the American republic were deeply influenced by Roman republican models.

high value on military background, political experience, personal connections, and oratorical ability. This basic outline of the structure of the republican system should not give the impression that it was inflexibly rigid. Like any political institution created by man, it could be modified by personality or circumstance. In the final era of the republic, the system proved to be difficult to adapt to the changing needs of the expanding empire. But on the whole it was remarkably resilient; it was the model that nearly all Western republics would look to for guidance in the modern period.

The ultimate authority of the state resided in the military. Originally its members had to be citizens; but as the empire expanded, recruits were taken from the provinces. The basic unit of organization was the Roman legion; it contained about forty-two hundred infantry and three hundred cavalry. Legions were further divided into centuries (one hundred men) commanded by centurions. To improve flexibility and maneuver, the legions were reorganized around 366 B.C. into "maniples," each of which contained two centuries. Military standards (*signa*) were carried by units in the field and were a source of pride; to lose one in battle was a significant humiliation. A commander in the field would deploy his infantry, slingers, archers, and cavalry as the terrain or his judgment dictated.

The secret of Roman military success was iron discipline. In an age when combat devolved into hand-to-hand engagements, the Roman legion operated as a cohesive body where its opponents most often did not. Roman men were raised from youth to respect authority and to develop manly virtue. Disobedience to lawful orders—even when the result was positive—could be brutally punished; according to legend, Titus Manlius Torquatus had his own son executed for insubordination. Punishments for cowardice or desertion were similarly brutal. Even high-ranking officers were not exempt. Sallust tells us that the field commander Turpilius, who escaped unharmed while his men were killed at the town of Vaga, was court-martialed, whipped, and then executed. (*Jug.* LXIX).

F. TRANSLATOR'S NOTE

Because Sallust sometimes sacrifices strict chronology in the interests of narrative unity, readers are encouraged to review the chronological tables before *Catiline* and *Jugurtha*. These provide a guide to the temporal flow of the action. The maps provide geographic orientation for places mentioned in the text. In the electronic edition of this book, footnotes can be accessed by clicking on each numbered footnote. The Latin texts of Sallust used in this translation are those found in Stuart, George *Sallust's Catiline and Jugurthine War*, New York: Hinds, Noble & Eldredge, 1905 and Sturgus, Minard *C. Crispi Sallustii Opera*, New York: D. Appleton & Co., 1872.

III. Maps And Illustrations

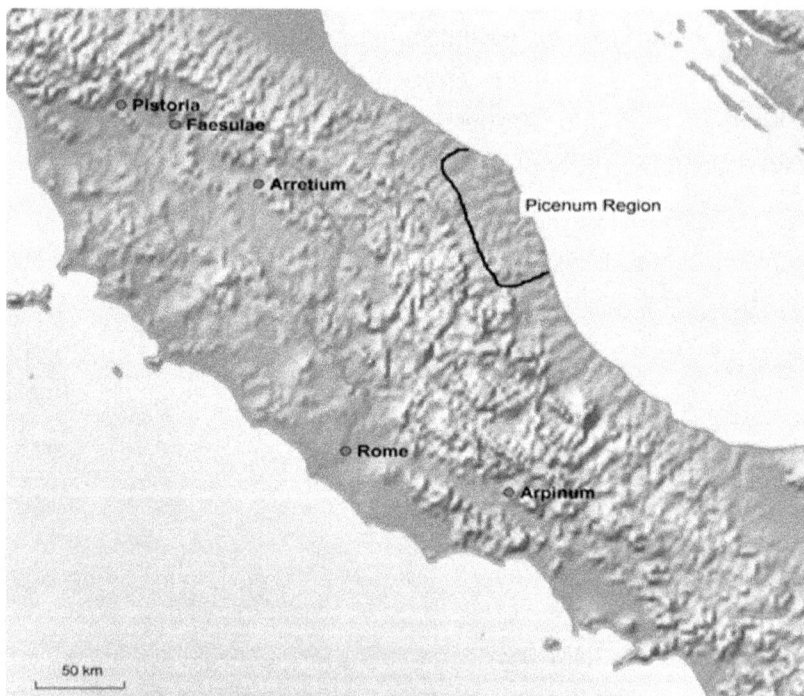

Central Italy at the time of Catiline's conspiracy, showing places mentioned in the text.

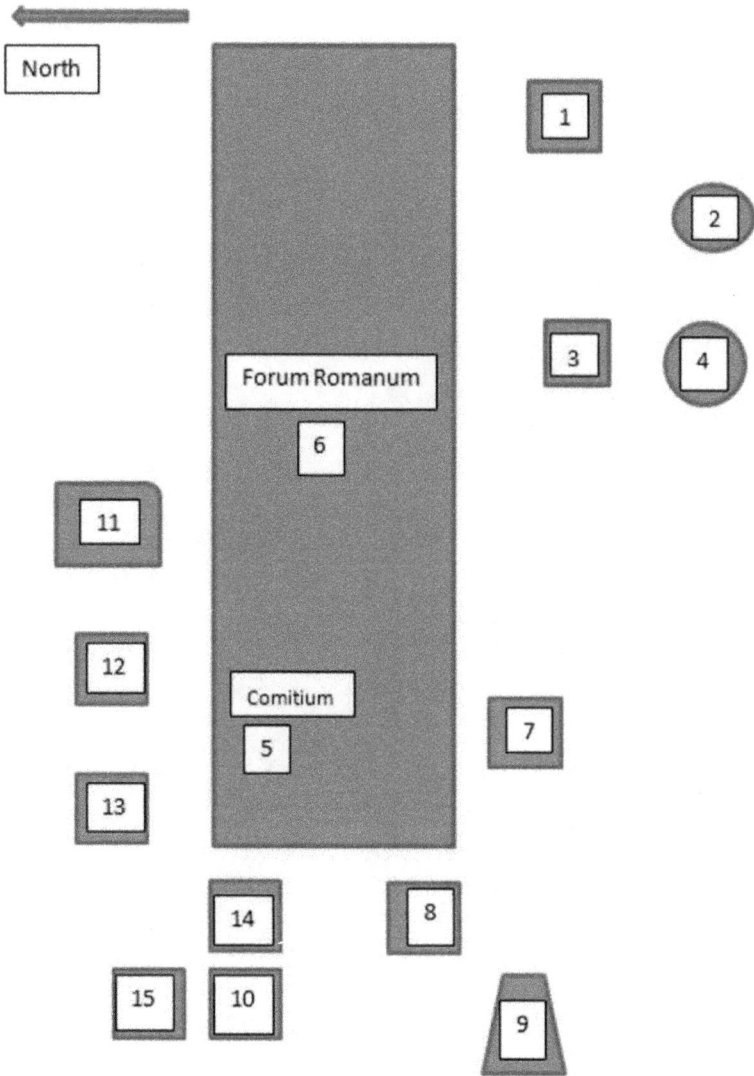

Major Landmarks Of The Roman Forum During The Republic

1. Regia	9. Schola Xantha
2. Aedes Vestae	10. Aedes Concordiae
3. Aedes Castoris	11. Basilica Aemilia
4. Fons Iuturnae	12. Basilica Porcia
5. Rostra	13. Curia
6. Lacus Curtius	14. Senaculum
7. Basilica Sempronia	15. Basilica Opimia
8. Templum Saturni	

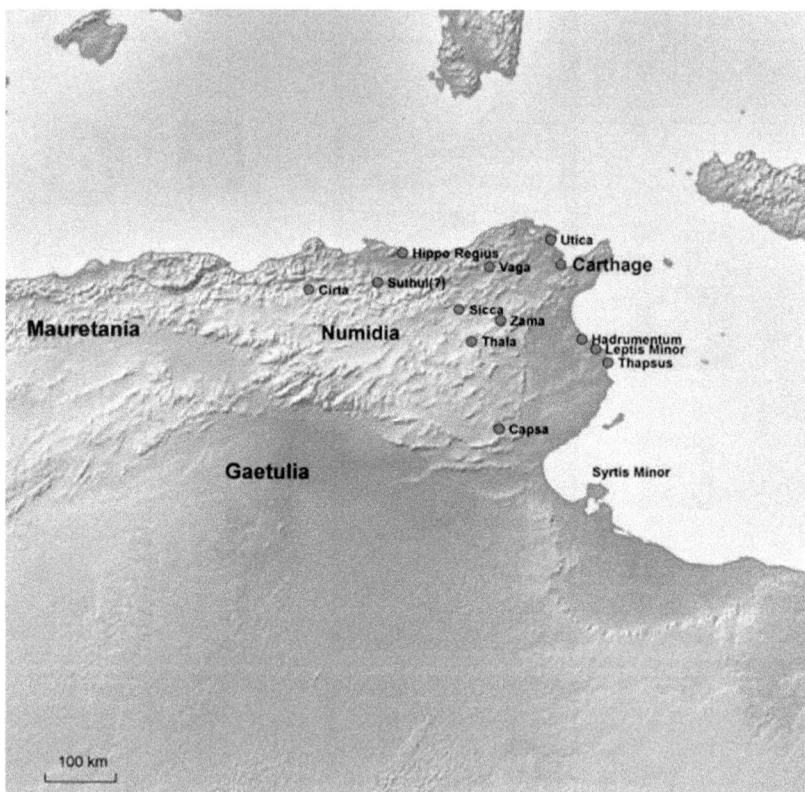

Numidia at the time of the Jugurthine War.

North Africa at the time of the Jugurthine War.

Modern Tunisian countryside. This was the kind of terrain in which the Jugurthine War was fought.

THE CONSPIRACY OF CATILINE

IV. CHRONOLOGY OF
THE CATILINIAN CONSPIRACY

YEAR (B.C.)	CONSULS IN OFFICE	IMPORTANT EVENTS
68	L. Caecilius Metellus, Q. Marcius Rex	Catiline serves as praetor.
67	C. Calpurnius Piso, M. Acilius Glabrio	Catiline serves as governor of Africa. Gabinian law passed.
66	M. Aemilius Lepidus, L. Volcatius Tullus	Manilian law passed .
65	L. Aurelius Cotta, L. Manlius Torquatus	Catiline prosecuted for *repetundae* (illegally acquired wealth). Catiline attempts his first conspiracy (murdering consuls), which fails.
64	L. Julius Caesar, C. Marcius Figulus	Catiline defeated in consular elections. Cicero and Caius Antonius elected.
63	M. Tullius Cicero, C. Antonius	The conspiracy takes final form. **Oct. 21**: Consuls given extraordinary powers to deal with crisis. **Oct. 27**: Manlius forms armed force at Faesulae in Etruria. **Oct. 28**: Consular elections.

		Catiline prosecuted by Lucius Paulus under the *Lex Plautia de vi*. ------------------------------------ **Nov. 6**: Conspirators meet at the house of Marcus Laeca. **Nov. 7(?)**: Failed assassination attempt against Cicero. **Nov. 8**: Cicero's first oration against Catiline. Catiline slips out of Rome. **Nov. 9**: Cicero's second oration against Catiline. Allobrogian legates become involved. **Mid-Nov.**: Catiline meets up with Manlius at Faesulae. ------------------------------------ **Dec. 3**: Cicero's third oration against Catiline. Conspirators in Rome arrested. **Dec. 5**: Cicero's fourth oration against Catiline. Conspirators sent to Tullianum prison and later executed. **Mid-Dec.**: Catiline learns of the capture and execution of his men in Rome.
62	Decimus Junius Silanus, L. Licinius Morena	Battle of Pistoria. Catiline killed in battle and his army destroyed.

V. Topical Organization Of *The Conspiracy Of Catiline*

TEXT SECTION(S)	TOPIC(S)
I-II	How man differs from the beasts. Why virtue is important. How power is transferred. The rise of greed. Qualities of a good life.
III-IV	The doing of great deeds. Being led astray from the right path. Why Sallust stayed out of power. Reason for writing history.
V-VI	Background and character of Catiline. Roman political development.
VII-VIII	Growth of corruption and decadence in Rome. Fortune is the master of all events.
IX-X	Virtues of the ancient Romans. How political events promoted the rise of immorality. The corrosive influence of greed.
XI-XII	Ambition and greed. The rise of Sulla and his negative influence. How wealth and riches became a substitute for honor.
XIII-XV	How evil habits corrupt the mind. Catiline was suited to the mores of the times. How Catiline corrupted the youth. Catiline's immoral background and personality.
XVI-XVIII	Catiline's golden opportunity. The people he recruited for his plans. Catiline's first conspiracy.

XIX-XXI	Cnaeus Piso sent to Spain.
	Catiline's speech to his henchmen.
	What Catiline's promises were.
XXII-XXIV	Ritualistic nature of the conspiracy.
	Fulvia betrays the plot.
	Catiline recruits more people.
XXV-XXVII	Nature of Sempronia.
	Catiline decides to run for consul.
	The meeting of conspirators at the house of M. Laeca.
XXVIII-XXXI	Assistance of Cornelius and Vargunteius.
	Manlius stirs up trouble in Etruria.
	Cicero's dilemma.
	Senate seeks information about the plot.
	Rome gripped by fear.
	Catiline tries to explain himself.
XXXII-XXXIV	Caius Manlius's message.
	Quintus Marcius's response.
XXXV-XXXVII	Quintus Catulus reads Catiline's letter in the senate.
	Roman people paralyzed about what to do.
XXXVIII-XL	General reasons for agitation against the state.
	The Allobrogian legates are recruited.
XLI-XLIII	Allobroges uncertain what to do.
	Events in Cisalpine and Transalpine Gaul.
	Lentulus prepares a force in Rome.
XLIV-XLVI	Allobroges contact other plotters.
	Letter of Lentulus to Catiline.
	Cicero arranges Volturcius's arrest and indicts the other conspirators.
XLVII-XLIX	Volturcius is interrogated and confesses.
	The Gauls confess.
	Testimony of Lucius Tarquinius.
	Attempt to implicate Caesar in the plot.
L-LII	Discussion on the conspirators' fate.
	Speech of Julius Caesar.
	Speech of Cato.
LIII-LV	Reaction to Cato's speech.
	The importance of character.
	Differing personalities of Caesar and Cato.
	Lentulus sent to the Tullianum prison and killed.

LVI-LVIII	Catiline forms his legions.
	Catiline learns of the capture and execution of his comrades in Rome.
	Catiline's speech to his men.
LIX-LXI	Catiline forms his units for battle.
	Marcus Petreius orders his men into action.
	The final defeat of Catiline's army.

VI. TEXT OF *THE CONSPIRACY OF CATILINE*

I. All men who seek to be better than the animals ought to exert themselves with the greatest efforts, lest they pass their lives in silence as if they were beasts of burden, which Nature has conditioned to be prostrate and subservient to their stomachs. All our powers are situated in our minds and bodies; we make use of the mind more for control, and the body for service. One of these we hold in common with the gods, and the other with the wild beasts. For me it seems more proper to seek glory through one's natural character than through the efforts of naked force and, since this life that we delight in is short, to fashion a legacy for ourselves that is as lasting as possible. For glory derived from riches and appearances is transitory and brittle, but masculine virtue is pure and eternal.

But for a long time it was disputed whether military prowess is derived more from physical ability or from strength of mind. Before embarking on an enterprise, one needs calculation; and after having calculated, timely action. Thus each of these factors, while inadequate alone, requires the other for assistance.

II. And so at first some kings—for monarchy was the first type of political authority—developed their characters, and others their bodies. The lives of men were lived without excessive greed; each was content with what he had. But later, when Cyrus in Asia and the Spartans and Athenians in Greece began to conquer cities and nations, and to make the lust for control an excuse for warfare, and to convince themselves that the greatest glory resided in the biggest empire: then finally through peril and hard experience it was learned that strong character is what is most useful in conflict.

If the strength of spirit of leaders and kings were as powerful in peace as it is in war, man's social affairs might have a more stable and constant quality; you would not perceive everything change and be stirred up in random fashion through conflict. For power is easily kept through the use of those techniques which were described above. However, when indolence replaces honest labor, and wantonness and arrogance replace continence and justice, one's fortune is likewise altered to fit these new manners. Thus power is always transferred from the less worthy to the most capable.

Men till the soil, sail the seas, and erect edifices. All these enterprises are subject to the principles of human character. But many men, having surrendered themselves to idle eating and sleeping, pass through life as wanderers, ignorant and uncultured; for them no doubt the body exists (contrary to Nature) for pleasure, and the soul remains a burden. For such people I consider their lives and deaths to be about equal, since neither state achieves any meaningful resonance. It seems to me, finally, that the spirit which truly lives and enjoys life is the one focused intensely on some productive business, and which seeks a reputation through great deeds or a noble calling. Yet in the great plenitude of life's pathways, nature reveals to one man one road, and to another man, a different one.

III. To perform good works for one's country is a beautiful thing; to speak well in her favor[15] is not out of place. One may become famous in peace or in war. Many of those who do important deeds (and who write about the acts of others) are praised. But to me, although equal glory does not follow from both the writing about and the doing of great things, nevertheless it is clear that writing about great events is among the most challenging of tasks. First, because the quality of the writing must

---

[15] I.e., through the use of rhetoric and oratory.

be equal to the events; and second, because when you hold people to account for their transgressions, readers believe your words are motivated by malice or envy. When you record the great virtue and glory of important personalities, the average man will accept the retelling with a ready frame of mind if he believes he himself could do the deeds easily. Anything beyond this he will consider false, or a gross exaggeration.

Like many others, I was led as a young man by my formative interests into the world of public affairs, and there found many things arrayed against me. Recklessness, bribery, and greed flourished at the expense of modesty, self-control and virtue. Although a proud soul rejects these sorts of evil practices, in the presence of so much vice my tender age was gripped by corrupt ambition. And although I dissented from the wayward behavior of others, still my longing for rewards harassed me with their same unwelcome notoriety and jealousy.

IV. So when my mind was finally free of these oppressive troubles and dangers, and I resolved to keep my distance from politics for the remaining years of my life, it was not my plan to fritter away my leisure in torpor and inactivity; neither was it my intention to take to farming or hunting, or to spend my time in servile activities. Instead I decided to go back to the plan that misplaced ambition had delayed my enthusiasm from commencing: to write a history of the Roman people, selecting the events that seemed worthy of record. I was ideally suited for this task, as my mind was then free of unrealistic expectations, fear and political rancor. Therefore I may acquit myself to write something, as accurately as I am able, on the conspiracy of Catiline; for I consider this event to be among the most memorable of crimes, due to the unusualness of the danger it presented. Some information must first be explained regarding his personal characteristics before I commence my narrative.

V. Lucius Catiline, born of a noble family, possessed a mind and body of great power, but also a deformed and wicked character.[16] From early manhood, civil war, killing, rapine and domestic discord were pleasing to him; and in these pursuits he cultivated his youthful years.[17] His body was tolerant of hunger, cold, and lack of sleep to a degree that exceeded any other man. He had a spirit that was audacious, deceitful, and shifting, agreeable in the role of both imitator and dissimulator; he was greedy for the possessions of others, lavish in his own habits, and fiery in his lusts. He had some eloquence, yet too little wisdom. His was an outsized and immoderate spirit, recognizing no boundaries, and always seeking the extremes.

After the end of the regime of Lucius Sulla, a great desire came over him to seize control of the state. He cared little by what methods he might seek this goal; he was prepared to consider whatever he needed provided it led to his own power. His arrogant spirit was agitated more and more every day by his lack of material possessions and knowledge of his evil inclinations; and he enlarged each of these conditions by the methods I have described above. He was further inspired by the corrupt morals of the republic, which was plagued by the insidious and separate diseases of luxury and greed.

As it has been relevant here to speak on the subject of public morals, so the context calls for a review and discussion of the domestic and military institutions of our ancestors, to examine how they formed our republic and of what quality it was when they willed it to us, and to discuss how, little by little, it changed from the best and grandest institution to the worst and most corrupt.

VI. From my understanding, the city of Rome was initially founded and inhabited by Trojan exiles wandering about with no

---

[16] His full name was Lucius Sergius Catilina. His great grandfather L. Sergius Silus served the state with distinction in the Second Punic War. Pliny, *Hist. Nat.* VII.29.

[17] He had taken part in Sulla's political purges. Seneca, *De ira* III.18.

fixed home and with Aeneas as their leader; with them were the Aborigines, an uncivilized people without laws or organized authority, free and unbound. These people later came together within the same city walls; they were of different origin and language, and living according to separate customs. They coalesced with remarkable facility; so in due course, a scattered and roving multitude was made a nation existing in domestic concord. But after the population, living standards, and territory increased, with prosperity and national strength becoming more evident, jealousy arose from opulence, as is often the case in human society. As a consequence kings and neighboring peoples tested them in war; scant few of their friends provided help, as the rest, stricken with fear, removed themselves from danger. The disciplined Romans made haste in domestic and military affairs, formed their plans, encouraged each other, and went out to confront their enemies; they protected their liberty, nation and parents by force of arms.

After warding off these dangers through martial virtue, they brought help to their allies and friends, and forged alliances more by giving benefits than receiving them. Their authority was based on law; and yet it bore the stamp of kings.[18] A chosen few, whose bodies were infirm with age but whose characters were fortified by wisdom, stepped in to advise the republic. These were called "fathers" either due to seniority or to the similarity of their cares. After the period of the monarchy—which at first had functioned to preserve liberty and augment the national welfare, then corrupted itself with arrogance and arbitrary authority—the form of government was changed, and two rulers were granted authority for one year. With this method they thought it least likely that human nature would grow haughty with license.

VII. Now at this time each man began more to advance his

---

[18] I.e., the form of government was a monarchy.

own fortunes and more to expose his character to public view. In the opinion of the kings, good men were more suspect than bad; the virtue of others was, for the kings, always something to be feared. But the state grew in power in an incredibly short amount of time once it had inherited political liberty. So much had the love of glory advanced. A young man, as soon as he was able to bear the rigors of military life, received instruction on military customs through labors in camp; he valued more the beauty of infantry weapons and the cavalry than the wanton indulgences of whore-chasing and dinner-parties.

For such men no type of labor was unfamiliar, nor any severe or arduous environment, nor any armed and intimidating enemy: for martial virtue permeated their very being. Their greatest competition for glory was among themselves. Each man hurried to slay an enemy or to climb over a wall, and to be seen while doing such a deed of valor. They held these actions to signify true wealth, and this to be the right kind of fame and lasting nobility. Eager for praise, they were generous with money; they sought decisive glory as well as honest riches. I could recall the locations where the Roman people routed a great number of enemies with relatively few soldiers, and the citadels fortified by natural geography that they captured by siege, were it not for the fact that such recollections would divert us too far from our topic.

VIII. Fortune is certainly the master of all events. She, more according to her pleasure than by objective merit, decides whether to elevate or to suppress all things. The deeds of the ancient Athenians, I believe, were distinguished and exceptional, but in truth somewhat less glorious than what posterity has conferred on them. But because writers of great talent flourished there, Athenian deeds are celebrated throughout the world as being without equal. Thus the value of those who accomplished great things is prized as highly as the distinguished talent of those able to praise them with words.

But this type of resource never existed for the Roman people; all of their most capable men were actively involved in other matters. No one sought to develop character without developing his body. The best men preferred to take action rather than to talk. They preferred rather that their own good deeds be praised by others than that they recount the exploits of strangers.

IX. So at home and in public good morals were cultivated; there was a surplus of harmony and a minimum of greed; and the right and the good prevailed for them not so much through law but by nature. Feuds, enmities, and discord were a matter for their enemies, while citizens instead contested with each other on the basis of virtue. They were conscientious in their offerings to the gods, thrifty in the household, and faithful to their friends. With these two arts—boldness in war and justice upon the advent of peace—they nurtured themselves and their republic.

I have a large amount of evidence to support this contention. In war, more often were those punished who attacked the enemy in violation of orders and who left the field of battle too late, than were those who relinquished their battle-standards, or dared to give ground after having been attacked. In peace, they exercised authority more by exchanges of benefits than by fear; and they preferred to overlook a received injury than to seek vengeance for it.

X. But when the republic grew through labor and the application of justice, and great kings had been subdued in war; when barbarous peoples and mighty nations were brought to heel; and when Carthage, jealous of the Roman Empire, was destroyed root and branch and every land and sea lay open; then, at last, Fortune began to vent her disfavor and all began to become turbulent. Those who had easily borne labors, dangers, insecurity and bitterness now found that leisure and riches—so desirable in some situations—were instead a burden and source of woe. Thus first the love of money grew, and then the love of power as well; these things were essentially the building blocks of all evils. Greed overturned honesty, good faith, and the other positive virtues; in their place it nurtured arrogance, cruelty, neglect of religious duty, and the idea that everything could be bought for a price.

Worldly ambition compelled many to become deceitful: to have one sentiment in the heart yet a different one ready on the tongue; to make friends and enemies not on an objective basis, but on an estimation of momentary convenience; and to display a good face rather than a good character. These tendencies grew little by little, occasionally to be punished. Afterwards, when the infection spread like a contagion, the state was transformed, and a government that was among the most just and strong became inhuman and unbearable.

XI. At first ambition rather than greed aroused the minds of men; even though it was a vice, it was still somewhat close to virtue. For men both good and bad long equally for glory, honor and power; but whereas one type advances by way of an honest path, the other relies on deceit and stratagems due to its deficiency of positive qualities of character. Greed carries with it a zeal for money, for which no wise man lusts. This greed, as if it were dipped in evil poison, makes a virile body and mind effeminate; it always is unbounded and insatiable, and neither surplus nor scarcity diminish it.[19]

But after Lucius Sulla took over the republic by force of arms, and things came to a miserable end after a good beginning, everyone began to plunder and to rob. Some coveted the homes of others, and some coveted their lands; the victors showed neither restraint nor discipline, carrying out odious and wicked acts against their fellows. To this was added the fact that Sulla, who had led his army into Asia, had—against the customs of our ancestors—indulged his forces with luxury and excessive liberality in order to secure their loyalty.

---

[19] Aulus Gellius (III.1) notes that obsessive pursuit of money causes men to neglect physical conditioning; this accelerates their corporeal decline.

Charming and sensual places easily enfeebled the spirits of warlike soldiers through leisure. Here the army of the Roman people first became accustomed to the pleasures of the flesh and excessive drink; to gaze in wonder on statues, paintings, and embossed vases; to pillage such artworks privately and publicly, to despoil houses of worship, and to violate all things sacred and profane. Thus these soldiers, after they had secured victory, left nothing for the defeated. As prosperity certainly fatigues the spirits of even the wise, persons of corrupted morals cannot be expected to restrain themselves in victory.

XII. After riches began to be considered a substitute for honor, and when glory, power, and force followed as a consequence, virtue grew feeble; humble circumstances were held a disgrace, and innocence began to be regarded with malice. As wealth grew steadily, luxury and greed combined with arrogance took possession of the youth. They freely took what they wanted, consumed with reckless abandon, and placed scant value on their own possessions while coveting those of others; shame, modesty, and all things human and divine were thought of as nothing. There was no sense of moderation.

It is worth the effort, when you examine the homes and villas constructed in the fashion of cities, to see the temples of the gods made by our most pious ancestors. Truly they adorned the homes of the gods with piety, and their own homes with glory; neither did they take anything away from their defeated enemies except their license to cause harm. In contrast, the modern individual— that most lazy of men—takes away, using the greatest treachery, everything from our allies that our strong, victorious ancestors left them. It is almost as if inflicting an injury were the same as the rightful exercise of power.

XIII. Why should I relate these things? They are credible to no one except those who have seen them: can mountains be cut through by groups of men, or can someone build on the sea?[20] For them their riches seem to have been a mockery; they might have made use of them reputably, yet they rushed to expend them indecently.

The lust for sex, gluttonous eating, and other frivolities advanced in no small way; men acted as women, and women uncovered their modesty; they combed land and sea to find culinary delicacies; they slept before their bodies needed sleep; they waited for neither hunger nor thirst, nor cold or exhaustion, but preempted all these things by their soft-living. These vices incited the youth to wrongdoing once their family resources had run out. A mind imbued with evil habits is not easily kept free from wantonness; and ever more immoderately, their minds had surrendered themselves to all varieties of material gain and profligacy.

XIV. In such a greatly corrupt nation it was an easy matter for Catiline to collect about himself an entourage of lackeys practiced in every type of crime and moral outrage: whatever profligate, adulterer, or glutton had wasted his family's legacy through misuse of his hands, stomach, or sexual organ; whoever had run up huge debts to make good some disgrace or illicit activity; all murderers and blasphemers from every walk of life convicted by the courts or fearing indictment for such actions; those whose hands and tongues were nourished by perjury or by the blood of their fellow citizens; and finally, all who were motivated by extreme poverty, disgrace, or a malicious conscience. All these character types were very close and dear to Catiline.

For if any innocent man initiated a friendship with him, he was made similar to Catiline's other flunkies by enticements and through daily contact with other members of his circle. But Catiline greatly longed for familiarity with the youth; their

---

[20] Referring to Xerxes.

48

unformed and pliable characters were seduced by his cunning without difficulty. Just as each man's interests burn differently according to age, Catiline offered prostitutes to some, and bought dogs and horses for others; finally he spared neither expense nor his own modesty while he made them loyal and beholden to himself. I understand that there were some who believed that the youths who visited Catiline's house were, in truth, not at all chaste. But this opinion prevailed more for other reasons than because anyone would have personally verified its accuracy.

XV. Even as a young man Catiline was involved in many nefarious escapades: with a virgin of good birth, with a Vestal priestess, and other affairs of various types that were against man-made and divine law.[21] At some point he became amorously infatuated with Aurelia Orestilla, who no good man ever praised except when it came to her beauty. When she hesitated to marry him due to fear of his adult stepson, it is understood by credible sources that he had the stepson killed in order to create an empty house for his wicked marriage. This seems to me to have been one of the primary causes for his ripening plot. His immoral soul, hostile to gods and men, was unable to find repose when awake or at rest: in such ways does conscience lay waste to a scheming mind. For this reason his visage was pale; his eyes had a sinister gaze, and he walked unevenly fast and slow. There was an entirely frenzied look in his face and expression.

XVI. But the youths whom he had enticed, as I have described above, he conditioned to commit criminal acts in a variety of ways. From this group he conditioned some to serve as false witnesses; he counted good faith, fortune, and personal danger as things of little consequence. And after he had ground down their reputations and senses of honor, he ordered even greater criminal acts.

---

[21] The Vestal priestess was Fabia Terentia, the sister of Cicero's wife Terentia.

If a reason for wrongdoing was not really at hand, he nevertheless assailed and killed the innocent as well as the guilty. Indeed, wanton evil and cruelty was for him preferable, lest the hands and minds of his pupils atrophy in leisure.

Because he had incurred huge debts in all parts of the world, and because a large number of Sulla's veteran soldiers—recalling their old memories of plunder and victories—longed for civil war, Catiline, trusting in these friends and allies, conceived the plan of overthrowing the government. There was no army in Italy. Gnaeus Pompeius was waging war at the ends of the earth.[22] Catiline himself nursed great hope for the consulship, and the senate was hardly watchful. Everything seemed secure and calm. This, in short, was Catiline's opportunity.

XVII. So, around the Kalends[23] of June during the consulships of Lucius Caesar and Caius Figulo, he first addressed his followers one by one. He exhorted and tested still others; he called attention to his own resources, the unpreparedness of the republic, and the great benefits of a conspiracy against the state. When he had reconnoitered as much as he wanted, he gathered together those who were most desperate and possessed the greatest audacity.

Appearing from the senatorial ranks were Publius Lentulus Sura, Publius Autronius, Lucius Cassius Longinus, Caius Cethegus, Publius and Servius Sulla, the sons of Servius, Lucius Vargunteius, Quintus Annius, Marcus Porcius Laeca, Lucius Bestia, and Quintus Curius. In addition, from the equestrian order

---

[22] He was campaigning in Syria at the time.

[23] That is, the beginning of June. Under the Roman calendar system, the first day of the month was known as the Kalendae. The name has its origin in the verb *calare*, "to call." This would traditionally have been the day on which the pontiff publicly indicated the results of his astronomical observations and the date of new moon.

were Marcus Fulvius Nobilior, Lucius Statilius, Publius Gabinius Capito, and Caius Cornelius. Besides these there were many settlers[24] and inhabitants of other municipalities, all of noble families. There was also a number of nobles whose involvement with the plot was more of a secret matter; they were more excited by the prospect of power than by material need or other necessity.

The majority of the remaining young men—but mostly those of noble backgrounds—favored Catiline's undertaking; in leisure they had the means to live sumptuously and without hardship, yet they preferred risk to predictability, and war to peace. At this time there were also those who thought that Marcus Licinius Crassus was not unaware of the conspiracy. Because Gnaeus Pompeius, his enemy, was leading a large army, he wanted to see anyone else's influence rise as a counterweight to him; at the same time he hoped that if the plot should succeed, he would easily be the key figure among them.[25]

XVIII. But before this time a few men had plotted against the republic; among them was Catiline. On that incident I will try to speak as accurately as I can. During the consulship of Lucius Tullus and Manius Lepidus, the newly-elected consuls Publius Autronius and Publius Sulla were indicted for bribery and suffered the penalties. A little while later, Catiline, found liable for recovery of extorted money,[26] was prohibited from seeking the consulship because he had been unable to declare his intention to

---

[24] "Settlers" meaning *coloniae*, or Roman colonists living in other parts of Italy. Although Rome was the dominant power on the peninsula, other regions still retained (as now) their local identities.

[25] That is, Crassus wanted to see another figure (Catiline) rise to prominence to act as a counterweight to Crassus's political rival, Pompey.

[26] Catiline had been a praetor in Africa and was accused of corruption by Publius Clodius. He apparently bribed his way out of the indictment.

run for the office within the required number of days.[27] At that same time there was a young man of noble birth, Cnaeus Piso, who was extremely audacious, needy, and unstable; his lack of resources and malignant character traits roused him to attack the republic.

Having communicated his plans to Catiline and Autronius around the fifth of December, they prepared to kill the consuls Lucius Cotta and Lucius Torquatus in the Capitol on the first of January.[28] Then, having taken the *fasces*, they would send Piso with an army to occupy the two territories in Spain.[29] When word of the plot leaked out they postponed their plans of murder until the fifth of February. Now they schemed not only to do harm to the consuls, but also to many senators. Had not Catiline rushed in signaling his allies in front of the Curia, on that day the worst outrage since the founding of Rome would have been committed; but because the number of armed men was not yet adequate, the plot collapsed.[30]

XIX. Afterwards, Piso—who was quaestor but had the authority of a praetor—was sent to Hither Spain with the help of Crassus, who knew him to be a dangerous antagonist of Cnaeus Pompeius. And neither had the senate sent him to the province unwillingly. Naturally, it wanted such a malevolent character far away from the heart of the republic; but at the same time, a good number of people from the upper classes thought of him as a

---

[27] This time period was 21 days, called a *trinundinum*.

[28] In the Roman calendar, *nona* represented the 7th of the month in March, May, July, and October. In other months it was the 5th. The *Kalenda* was the first of each month.

[29] The *fasces lictoriae* are well-known symbols of Roman judicial authority, carried by lictors. They were bound bundles of wooden rods with an axe in the middle.

[30] See the "Chronology of Events" table above for the dating of this "first conspiracy" and for the dates of the consulships named here.

security bulwark, for even at that time Pompey's power was menacing. Now this Piso was killed by his Spanish cavalry while leading a march in the province.

There are those who say that the barbarians were unable to tolerate his unjust domineering, arrogance, and cruelty; others maintain that his cavalry, who were Pompey's veterans and faithful to their former commander, attacked Piso at Pompey's recommendation. Never before were Spaniards known to have carried out such an act; in fact they had borne brutal discipline often in the past. We will leave this matter an unsettled question. Regarding the first conspiracy, enough here has been said.

XX. When Catiline considered the men before him whom I have just mentioned, although he had often spoken to them separately, nevertheless, believing he should call them all together to encourage them, he brought them to a secluded part of his estate. Having removed all witnesses away to a safe distance, he made the following remarks:

"Had I not already observed your bravery and loyalty, a great opportunity would have come about in vain. Great hopes and power would be in my hands to no avail; and neither would I strive for something uncertain over what is certain with the help of idlers or unreliable characters. But because I have become aware, through numerous and great hardships, of your steadfastness and loyalty to me, my mind has been prepared to take on a surpassing and historic mission. At the same time, I realize we are in agreement on what is considered good and bad. For to want—and not to want—the same thing is, at last, the definition of a robust friendship.

"All of you have previously heard from me separately regarding what I have been turning over in my mind. And as the days go by, my mind is more set ablaze when I consider what the condition of our lives may be, unless we ourselves act to claim our liberty. After the republic relinquished power and legal authority to the hands of a few, it is always to them that kings and

53

tetrarchs are financially obligated,[31] and to them that peoples and nations must pay tribute. All the rest of us—vigorous, brave men both noble and common—were the masses, without a voice, without authority, and submissive to those to whom—if a real republic existed—we should be seen as formidable.

"Thus all influence, power, public offices and wealth are under their direct control, or where they want them to be. They leave for us the risks, humiliations, adverse court rulings, and privations. How long will you tolerate this, you great men? Is it not better to die as virtuous men, than to fritter away a shameful and miserable existence as the laughingstock of arrogant mediocrities? Beyond all doubt—and by the trust in gods and men—victory is in our hands. We are of a healthy age, and our spirits are strong; the others have decayed as a result of their advanced years and wealth. What is needed is a first step; all else will follow from this.

"What mortal man of virile character can tolerate the fact that these people hoard all the riches, that they squander them in building on the sea and leveling mountains,[32] while our families lack the basic necessities? Should they stitch together two or even more houses, and we possess not even a hearth?[33] They buy paintings, statues, and carved artworks; they pull down new buildings and build others; they finally acquire and abuse their money by whatever methods possible. Still, in the grip of such wantonness, they are unable to master their wealth. We have poverty inside the home, debt beyond the threshold, bleak

---

[31] The text here literally means owing *vectigales*, or taxes. The word *tetrarchae* (tetrarch) here has its archaic meaning, that of a subordinate prince.

[32] A reference to Roman engineering projects involving the building of artificial harbors and structures in the mountains.

[33] The word *Lar* is used here, which is the name of the tutelary god of home and hearth.

prospects, and even more bitter hopes. What do we have that remains except a miserable soul?

"Will you wake up, then? Know that this, *this* represents the freedom you have wished for, as well as the riches, distinction, and glory seen by the eyes of the world. Fortune presents all these rewards to the victors. The quest, the moment in time, the danger, the necessity, and the great spoils of war urge you forward more than any words of mine. Make use of me either as a leader or a regular soldier: neither my mind nor my body will hesitate in full devotion to your cause. These things, I hope, I will accomplish with you as consul, unless perhaps my feelings are mistaken, and you are more prepared to be subservient than to rule."

XXI. When men who were weighed down by all types of miseries (and who had neither resources nor any prospects) heard these words, and although to them overturning the established order seemed greatly valuable in itself, still many of them demanded that Catiline explain what the conditions would be for war, what spoils they might acquire by arms, what sort of resources and chances they might have, and where they might find them.

Then Catiline promised the discharge of debts, proscriptions[34] for the elites, judgeships, priesthoods, plunder, and everything else that war and passion deliver to the victor. He also said that Piso was in Hither Spain and Publius Sittius Nucerinus in Mauretania with his army, both of them being participants in the conspiracy; that Caius Antonius (whom he hoped would be his co-conspirator) sought the consulship, and happened to be a close friend of his who was enmeshed by all sorts of obligations;[35] and that with him in the consulship, he would activate the plot.

---

[34] I.e., targeted executions.
[35] Meaning that he would be easy to manipulate because of his financial and other burdens.

At this point he spewed out abuse on every man of good name, and praised each of his own men individually. He reminded one man of his insolvency, another of his greed, several of peril and disgrace, and many of Sulla's victory, which had yielded much plunder. After he saw that everyone's spirits were stirred, he encouraged them to keep his candidacy in mind; he then dismissed the gathering.

XXII. There have been those who say that Catiline, having finished his speech, passed around a bowl of human blood mixed with wine in order to bind by solemn oath his associates in crime. When, after the curse,[36] everyone had drunk a little of it—as customarily happens in sacred rituals—he revealed his plan. He is believed to have done this with the idea that their trust in each other would be greater if they shared knowledge of the crime. Some consider this story and many other details besides to be the inventions of those who thought that the hostility against Cicero which arose afterwards would be assuaged by pointing out the barbarity of those whom he punished.[37] For the historian, however, too little is known with certainty about something of this significance.

XXIII. Involved also in the conspiracy was one Quintus Curius, a man of reasonably good origins yet compromised by scandal and criminal acts: the censors had removed him from the senate on account of his conduct. He possessed no less vanity than he did recklessness. He could neither refrain from repeating the things he heard nor conceal even his own crimes. He was entirely without consideration for what he said or did.

Associated with him was an aristocratic woman named Fulvia,

---

[36] The curse referenced in the preceding paragraph, when Catiline heaped abuse on "men of good name."

[37] Cicero eventually had key participants in the conspiracy executed. It was a controversial decision that met with some public disfavor.

with whom he carried on an extended affair. As financial hardship made him less able to provide her an extravagant lifestyle, he became less appealing to her; he then suddenly switched to bluster and took to promising her the seas and mountains,[38] while also threatening her now and then with physical violence[39] unless she submitted to him. Ultimately he became much more aggressive than he previously had been.

But Fulvia, having learned the reason for Curius's strange behavior, decided that such a danger to the republic should not remain unexposed; so without divulging the name of the participant in Catiline's conspiracy, she passed on to a number of people the things she had heard about it. This revelation in particular stirred up a general feeling to bestow the consulship on Marcus Tullius Cicero. For in fact most of the nobility seethed in jealousy before this, and considered the office of consul practically "polluted" if it were obtained by a "new man," however exceptional he might be.[40] But when danger made its appearance, envy and haughtiness were eclipsed.

XXIV. Once the elections took place, Marcus Tullius[41] and Caius Antonius were pronounced consuls. This fact greatly unsettled the members of the conspiracy. Neither did Catiline's mania diminish; it mounted in intensity by the day. He procured arms at favorable places throughout Italy and transported borrowed money (his own or that obtained by the credit of

---

[38] A colloquial expression (*maria montesque polliceri*).

[39] The text uses the colorful expression *minari interdum ferro*, literally "to threaten now and then with iron" with "iron" meaning the cold steel of a blade.

[40] A "new man" (*novus homo*) was a man not of noble origin who was the first to serve in the senate. We can well imagine that the phrase was used as an aristocratic sneer at non-patrician aspirants to political office.

[41] Cicero.

associates) to Faesulae[42] in the care of someone named Manlius, who later was the first in the ranks when the war came to be fought.

At this time he is said to have won over a large number of men of all types, and even a few women. The women at first tolerated the sexual sale of their bodies because of the vast expenses they had incurred; later, when advancing age encroached on their profits but not on their taste for luxury, they became deeply mired in debt. Through them Catiline believed he could incite the urban slaves to rebel and burn Rome; he planned then either to compel the women's husbands to join him or, failing that, to kill them.

XXV. But among these conspirators was Sempronia, who had often carried out many crimes with virile confidence. In upbringing and appearance—as well as in her spouse and children—this woman was blessed; educated in Greek and Latin literature, she also danced and played the cithara more capably than decorum permitted. She possessed many other capabilities that are the tools of extravagance. For her anything was more valuable than feminine virtue and chastity; you could not easily tell whether she showed less consideration for her money or her honor. Once her passion was kindled, she more often pursued men than was pursued by them.

Earlier in life she had often projected a false honesty, had refused to pay her creditors, and had even been involved in murder; she was brought to the edge of the abyss by both poverty and luxury. Still, her character was not entirely uncouth: she could compose poetry and amuse listeners with her wit; in speech she could be alternately modest, pliable, or brazen. In short, she possessed much charm and humor.

---

[42] Faesulae (modern Fiesole) was an ancient Etrurian town about 3 miles from the modern city of Florence. It was located on a hill above the valley of the Arnus. *See* Livy XXII.3.

XXVI. These preparations having been completed, Catiline nevertheless sought the office of consul in the following year, hoping that if he was elected, he might easily be able to use Antonius for his purposes. But he was not idle during this time; in every way he laid the groundwork for treachery against Cicero. The requisite guile and cunning in avoiding these machinations were not missing from Cicero's personality, either. For in fact from the beginning of his consulship he had, by means of various promises made through Fulvia, caused Quintus Curius—whom I mentioned earlier—to reveal to him Catiline's plot.

To this end he prevailed on his colleague Antonius, by means of an agreement on a province,[43] not to foment designs against the republic. He also secretly arranged to surround himself with the personal protection of friends and fellow citizens. After the day of the elections came, and neither Catiline's candidacy nor the schemes he had drawn up against the consuls in the campus[44] had ended successfully, he resolved to use naked force and push things to the outermost limits, since what he had tried to do secretly ended in bitterness and humiliation.

XXVII. Therefore he sent Caius Manlius to Faesulae and this part of Etruria, a man named Septimius of Camerinum to Picenum[45] and Caius Julius to Apulia; others went to other places, wherever he believed they might be most needed for his plans. Meanwhile at Rome he simultaneously undertook many

---

[43] A Roman law dating from the time of Caius Gracchus held that each co-consul would be assigned a province. Cicero initially received Macedonia, and Antonius received Cisalpine Gaul. Macedonia was a richer province, so Cicero offered to trade provinces with Antonius in return for his support.

[44] The Campus Martius, an area of land north of the Capitoline Hill about two square kilometers in size. It was filled with large public buildings and temples.

[45] A region of ancient Italy between the Apennines and the Adriatic where the modern region of Marche is now located. *See* Strabo V.4.1.

preparations: setting ambushes for the consuls, planning arson attacks, and taking possession of strategic places with armed men. He himself was armed and ordered others to be as well. He urged his men always to be attentive and ready; he worked feverishly day and night and was constantly vigilant, being overcome neither by lack of sleep nor unrelenting labor.

Finally, when nothing came of these many efforts, again in the dead of night he called together the conspiracy's principals at the residence of Marcius Porcius Laeca. Reciting a litany of complaints about their faintheartedness, he then pointed out that he had sent Manlius to take charge of the force which had prepared to take up arms, that others had been sent to various strategic places and were preparing to wage war, and that he himself wanted to depart for the armed force if he could first overthrow Cicero, who had so far blocked all of his plans.

XXVIII. Many were fearful and confused at this point; but Caius Cornelius, a Roman knight, pledged his assistance along with the senator Lucius Vargunteius. That night they decided to pay a presumptively official visit to Cicero along with a team of armed men and, taking him by surprise, murder him in his own house. When Curius learned of the magnitude of the danger that was imminent to the consul, he conveyed to Cicero the details of the developing treachery using Fulvia as an intermediary. Thus the plotters, having been barred admission to the residence, undertook their scheme in vain.

Meanwhile Manlius in Etruria began to stir up the common people, a task made easier by their extreme poverty, anguish at past injustice, and desire for a change of the current state of affairs: during Sulla's regime, they had lost their lands and other possessions of value. He also solicited the support of bandits of various types, of which there were a large number in this region; he even made use of some of Sulla's ex-colonists who, due to their dissoluteness and lack of restraint, had nothing remaining of the plunder they once possessed.

XXIX. When these developments were conveyed to Cicero he became much distressed by the twin dangers he faced: he was neither able to protect the city against the conspirators' machinations much longer, nor able to acquire any first-hand knowledge as to the size and objective of Manlius's army. He thus referred the matter to the senate, which had already been disturbed by public rumors. The senate therefore ordered—as often happens in matters involving violence—that the consuls should take appropriate measures to ensure that the republic not be harmed.

By Roman custom, this power is the greatest given by the senate to a magistrate; it allows the raising of an army, the waging of war, the coercion of allies or citizens by any means, and the possession of ultimate power and jurisdiction in domestic and military matters. Unless these powers are given by order of the people, the consul otherwise has no right to them.[46]

XXX. A few days later senator Lucius Saenius read aloud before the senate a letter he said had been delivered to him from Faesulae; the letter alleged that Caius Manlius had taken up arms with a large force on the twenty-seventh of October.[47] At the same time, as often happens in such situations, some observers reported omens and portents; others alleged meetings, the movement of weapons, and slave uprisings at Capua and in Apulia.

So by the decree of the senate, Quintus Marcius Rex was sent

---

[46] The reference is to the *senatus consultum ultimum* ("SCU") or "Final Act." This is the modern name given to a senatorial decree in the late republic that conferred special powers on a magistrate in times of emergency. It effectively replaced the outmoded practice of appointing a dictator.

[47] The date given in the text is *VI Kalendas Novembris*. To convert this Roman calendar date to the Gregorian calendar, we must add 2 to the number of days in the preceding month (October), and then from this subtract the date in question. Thus $31 + 2 - 6 =$ October 27. The adjustment is slightly different for dates in *Nonae* and *Idus*. See Greenough, J. B. (ed.), *Allen & Greenough's New Latin Grammar*, Newburyport: Focus Publishing (2000), p. 422.

to Faesulae and Quintus Metellus Creticus[48] to Apulia and its vicinity. Each of these men were military commanders just outside Rome, blocked from celebrating triumphs by the false pretexts of a few persons whose habit it was to sell for a price everything honest and dishonest. The praetors Quintus Pompeius Rufus and Quintus Metellus Celer were sent to Capua and the Picene region respectively, with instructions to raise an army appropriate for the crisis and the danger.

The senate also made provision for a reward to anyone providing information on the conspiracy against the republic: one hundred thousand sesterces and his freedom (if a slave), and two hundred thousand sesterces with an amnesty if the informant had any involvement in the affair. The senate also directed that gladiatorial units be distributed at Capua and other municipalities according to their ability to support them; that watches be stationed throughout the entire city of Rome under the supervision of subordinate magistrates.

XXXI. The republic was alarmed by these measures, and the appearance of the city changed. From the summits of happiness and frivolity—which an extended peace had begotten—suddenly a consuming dread intruded. The public was agitated, apprehensive, trusting little in any specific location or person, and was neither fighting war nor enjoying peace;[49] each man gauged the level of danger by the counsel of his own fears. The power of our republic had made the women unaccustomed to the anxiety of approaching war; they beat their bodies in hysteria, raised their hands skyward in prayer, fretted over their small children, asked

---

[48] He attained the surname Creticus for his effective service on the island of Crete.

[49] I.e., they were apprehensive because they were in a state of limbo between war and peace.

ceaseless questions, and reacted with terror to every rumor they could seize hold of. Abandoning pride and frivolous pastimes, they grew despondent about themselves and their country.

But Catiline's hard-hearted soul continued along the same course, even though armed detachments were being raised and he had been indicted by Lucius Paulus under the Plautian Law.[50] Finally, in order to cover his tracks with lies or to exculpate himself (as if he had been the victim of others' slander), he made an appearance in the senate. The consul Marcus Tullius—either from fear of Catiline's presence or from anger generated by outrage—then delivered a brilliant oration, which he later published, that was very much to the republic's advantage.[51]

Once seated, Catiline was prepared to lie about everything. With his face hanging low, and taking on a supplicating tone of voice, he started to ask the other senators not to believe anything too rashly. He said he had come from a good family, and from earliest youth had so arranged his life that he had nothing but good things to look forward to. They should not think that a man of his patrician background—who like his ancestors had been of such service to the Roman people—would seek the downfall of the republic, while Marcus Tullius, who was little more than a tenant in the city of Rome, could be its guardian.[52] When he was about to add more taunts, all the other senators raised their voices loudly against him, calling him an enemy of the state and a traitor. He then shouted back at them furiously, "Because I'm now hemmed

---

[50] This civil security law (*Lex Plautia de vi*) apparently dated from 89 B.C. and was authored by the tribune Marcus Plautius Silvanus.

[51] The "Marcus Tullius" referred to here is of course Cicero. The speech is the famous "First Oration Against Catiline," a masterpiece of invective.

[52] This was a patrician snub of Cicero's background as a *novus homo* (first in his family to serve in the senate or be elected consul) from a modest equestrian family.

in and pushed to the edge of the abyss by my enemies, I'll put out my fire with demolition."[53]

XXXII. Finally he rushed home from the Curia.[54] There he turned over in his mind many of the recent events; for his plots against the consul had come to nothing, and he realized that the city was protected from arson attack by patrols. Believing the best course of action was to augment his army and secure, before the legions were formally drawn up, the many necessities that might be needed for war, he set out for Manlius's camp with a few other men in the dead of night. But to Cethegus, Lentulus, and a few others whom he knew were eager to display their audacity, he ordered that they increase the influence of their cell by whatever means they could; they should ripen their plans against the consul, prepare for assassinations, arson attacks, and other acts of war. He said that he himself would march on the city at a not-too-distant time with a large army.

While these things were transpiring at Rome, Caius Manlius sent a few delegates from his force with instructions to convey the following:

XXXIII. "Both gods and men bear witness, commander, that we have neither taken up arms against our country nor created perils for others, but rather have acted to protect ourselves personally from harm. We are miserable and in dire need; many of us are alienated from our country by the violence and cruelty of the usurers, and all have lost their reputations and property. None of us was permitted—as was the habit of our ancestors—to have access to the law so that we, having lost our patrimony, might enjoy the benefits of being free men. Such was the barbarity of the moneylenders and the praetor.

---

[53] A threat to cause violence. The reference is to the technique of fighting fires by demolishing buildings to deprive a spreading fire of fuel.

[54] The meeting house of the Roman senate.

"Often your ancestors, taking pity on the average Roman, brought relief to his poverty by passing decrees. Most recently in our memory, because of the magnitude of the debt involved, silver was paid back in copper coin with the consent of the wealthy classes. Often the same plebians, either animated by a desire to rule or offended by the arrogance of the judges, have rebelled from the patricians. We seek neither power nor riches—which are the source of war and rivalry among people—but freedom, which no good man gives up except with his breath of life. We respectfully ask you and the senate, after having deliberated about your miserable fellow citizens, to restore the rule of law, which the injustice of the praetor violated. We ask that you not force us to seek out how our blood may be most usefully expended."

XXXIV. Quintus Marcius responded to this by saying that anyone who wished to petition the senate for redress should first lay down his arms and make his way to Rome as a penitent. The senate of the Roman people had always possessed such compassion and benevolence that no one had ever sought aid from it in vain.

But along his march Catiline sent letters to many men of consular rank as well as to some well-placed nobles. He said that because he was surrounded by bogus accusations and unable to deal with the extreme partisanship of his enemies, he would yield to Fortune and set out for exile in Massilia:[55] not because he was in any way guilty of a crime, but so that the republic would be at peace, and that no strife might arise from his fighting the charges. Yet in the senate Quintus Catulus read a quite different letter that, he claimed, had been delivered to him in Catiline's name. The text of the letter is given below.

XXXV. "*Lucius Catiline to Quintus Catulus.*[56] Being aware of your exceptional loyalty—most welcome to me in my present

---

[55] Modern Marseilles in the south of France.
[56] This is the letter's salutation.

dangers—generates faith in my communication. For this reason I have decided to offer no justification for my new decision. I have decided to offer my reasons out of no guilty conscience, but so that you may be permitted to know the truth, as I call heaven to witness.

"Disturbed by insults and abusive behavior and deprived of the fruits of my labor and diligence, I was unable to maintain a position of dignity. I took up the cause of the dispossessed as my general practice, not because I was unable to pay my debts out of my own funds and assets (the generosity of Orestilla could certainly satisfy the debts of many using her own and her daughter's resources), but because I was seeing unworthy men adorned with accolades, and noticed that I was alienated from others due to false suspicions.

"I have tried to seek an honorable course in my current situation in the hope of preserving my remaining dignity. Whenever I wish to explain more, someone announces that I am to be met with violence. I now deliver Orestilla to you, entrusting her to your good faith. In the name of your children, I implore you to guard her from injury. Farewell."

XXXVI. Catiline lingered with Caius Flaminius in the region of Arretium for a few days, distributing arms to a region previously stirred up by his agitation; he then sought to join Manlius in his camp, bringing with him the fasces and other insignia of power. When these events became known in Rome, the senate declared Catiline and Manlius to be outlaws; it gave the rest of the group a day as amnesty, during which they might disarm without retribution (except those convicted of capital crimes). It also ordered that the consuls should begin conscription;[57] that Antonius with his army should move quickly against Catiline; and that Cicero should remain at Rome with a garrison force.

---

[57] I.e., in order to raise a military force to confront the danger.

It was during this time, I believe, that the power of the Roman people appeared to be most pathetic. From where the sun rose to where it set, the conquered world yielded to Rome's arms; at home leisure and riches abounded, which mortal man holds so dear. Nevertheless there were citizens who, because of their warped characters, passionately sought to destroy both themselves and their republic. For even with the issuance of the two senatorial decrees, no one in the entire group was induced by financial reward either to betray the conspiracy or desert Catiline's camp. Such was the power of the disease, and to such an extent had decay rotted the minds of so many of our citizens.

XXXVII. This destructive way of thinking was found not only in those who were participants in the conspiracy, but also entirely with the common citizenry, which gave its assent to Catiline's undertakings out of a desire for change in the present state of affairs. In this fashion the public certainly seemed to behave. For in every state those who have no resources envy the productive citizens, praise the dregs, hate the traditional, pine for novelties and, due to dissatisfaction with their own lot, are eager for everything to be changed. They are nourished by upheaval and sedition without care, as poverty is easily maintained without great expense.

But the headlong rush of the urban denizens into danger was due to many causes. First of all, those who distinguished themselves by shameless behavior and depravity, as well as those who had lost their inheritances by frivolous spending, and finally all whom scandal or crime had driven from their homes: all flowed into Rome as if it were an open sewer. Besides this, many were mindful of Sulla's victories, when they had seen some from the ranks of common soldiers become senators and others achieve such riches that allowed them to enjoy the food and life of a king. Each man hoped for such an outcome if he took up arms.

In addition, the youth who had endured poverty through physical labor in the countryside preferred—aroused by public and private welfare—urban leisure to thankless rural toil. These types, along with all the others, augmented the public evils. It is hardly surprising that men who were destitute, marked by bad character, and full of unrealistic hopes would have shown the same level of consideration for their country as they did for themselves.

Those who had their parents proscribed after Sulla's victory, who had lost their possessions or had their liberties impaired, certainly looked forward to the onset of war with a purposeful spirit. Furthermore, those who were part of a faction other than that of the senate preferred to see the republic thrown into chaos than have their own power diminished. This was the great evil which had reappeared in the state after so many years.

XXXVIII. After the power of the tribunes had been restored in the consulship of Gnaeus Pompeius and Marcus Crassus, some young men attained the pinnacle of power. They were at a rebellious stage in life and had defiant dispositions; they stirred up the lower classes by denouncing the senate, later raising expectations ever higher with public hand-outs and promises designed to make themselves influential and respected. Against these people the majority of the nobility struggled with all its power, using the prestige of the senate for its own importance. And if I may sum up the matter briefly, anyone after that time who agitated against the state made use of grandiose principles: some claimed they were defending the rights of the people, others that they were safeguarding the preeminence of the senate. Pretending to care about the public good, each side fought for its own political power. Neither of them had any sense of restraint or wisdom in resolving differences; and both enforced victory with animalistic savagery.

XXXIX. But when Gnaeus Pompeius was sent to conduct the maritime war and the Mithridatic War, the influence of the lower classes lessened while the power of the elites gathered force.[58] These had control of the civil magistracies, the provinces, and everything else. They were invulnerable and rich, and lived their lives without fear; they intimidated others by their control of the law, through which they directed the masses more peacefully using the judicial bench.

But when the expectation for change produced uncertainties, old quarrels kindled the minds of political opponents. If in his first battle Catiline had marched off the field victorious—or if he merely fought to a draw—great disaster and upheaval would have visited the republic; and even those who had won would not have been able to make use of their victory for long. Exhausted and bled white, they would have had their power and liberty wrested away by someone stronger than they.

Nevertheless, there were a good number of people outside the conspiracy who went over to Catiline's side when the fighting started. Among them was a senator's son named Fulvius: his father ordered him to be executed after he had been brought back from his adventure. At the same time Lentulus, just as Catiline had ordered, was soliciting either personally or through agents anyone he thought suitable (either from personality or circumstances) for the grand scheme;[59] he approached not only citizens, but whatever type of man who might be useful in armed conflict.

XL. He therefore ordered Publius Umbrenus to meet

---

[58] In 67 B.C. a law was passed (the *Lex Gabinia*) that gave Pompey power to conduct military operations against pirates which then infested parts of the Mediterranean. Pompey waged it successfully. The war against Mithridates VI (the king of Pontus) referred to here was the so-called Third Mithridatic War, lasting from 75 to 63 B.C. Pontus was located in Asia Minor.

[59] Sallust's phrase here is *novis rebus*, which literally indicates a "new thing" or "new order."

representatives of the Allobroges[60] and ask—if possible—whether they would join in a military pact. Supposing that they were weighed down with public and private debt, and because the Gauls were also by nature a warlike people, he thought they could easily be added to the conspiracy. Because he had done business in Gaul, Umbrenus was known by many of the leading figures of their states and he in turn knew them. So when he first saw their delegation in the forum, without delay he inquired a bit about the state of their country and its current plight, showing some sympathy for their situation; he then asked what solution they sought for their problems. After he heard them complain about the greed of the magistrates, accuse the senate of doing nothing to help them, and say they expected death to be the cure for their misery, he told them, "If you wish to be true men, I will show you a rational plan through which you may escape these ills."

When he said this the Allobroges were inspired by the greatest hopes and, so induced, they pleaded with Umbrenus to take pity on them. Nothing was so drastic or difficult that they could not cheerfully do it, provided that it would liberate their country from the burden of debt. He led them to the house of Decimus Brutus, which was near the Forum and not unconnected with the conspiracy because of the involvement of Sempronia; at this time Brutus was absent from Rome. He then fetched Gabinius, so that a greater impression would come from the presentation. Once he was present he revealed the conspiracy, identified its members, and finally—so that the delegates' courage might swell that much more—named many innocent men of all backgrounds.[61]

XLI. But for a considerable time the Allobroges were not sure what decision they should take. On one hand were the debt issue,

---

[60] The Allobroges were a Gallic tribe located roughly between Lake Geneva, the Isere River, and the Rhone.

[61] That is, he exaggerated the size of the conspiracy to try to impress the Allobroges as potential recruits.

their enthusiasm for war, and the great benefits coming from the expectation of victory; on the other hand were the powerful resources of the senators and the safety of inaction, a certain reward rather than a doubtful hope. These issues they turned over many times until Fortune decided the matter in favor of the republic. They thus revealed everything they had learned to Quintus Fabius Sanga, whose patronage their country had made great use of. Cicero, after learning of the plot from Sanga, ordered the Allobrogian legates to feign strong enthusiasm for the conspiracy, make contact with its other participants and extend them assurances, then apply themselves as much as possible to verify the plotters' culpability.

XLII. At about this same time, events had been taking place in Cisalpine and Transalpine Gaul,[62] as well as in the regions of Picenum, Bruttium, and Apulia. Those whom Catiline had sent out ahead were acting altogether recklessly and nearly as if they were demented. Through their nocturnal meetings, open displays of military hardware and weapons, and heightened levels of movement and activity, they generated more fear than actual danger. The praetor Quintus Metellus Celer, having learned of the involvement of a few of their number, clapped them into prison using a senatorial decree. The same thing was done in Cisalpine Gaul by Caius Murena, who was overseeing this province as legate.

XLIII. At Rome, Lentulus with some other key members of the conspiracy prepared (as it seemed to him) a large force, so that when Catiline came to the vicinity of Faesulae with his army, the tribune of the people Lucius Bestia could summon an official meeting and lodge a complaint about Cicero's actions. In this way he could impose on the great consul the onus of a most serious conflict. With this signal the rest of the band of plotters would

---

[62] The phrase used here is *in Gallia citeriore atque ulteriore.*

implement each of their individual plans on the following night.

Their responsibilities were said to have been divided in this way. Statilius and Gabinius with a large group were to light fires at twelve vital points in the city simultaneously, so that in the confusion it would be easier to lay hands on the consul and others against whom they had planned their treacherous attacks. Cethegus would blockade Cicero's front door and then seize him by force, while other conspirators would do the same to different officials. The sons of some families (the majority of which were from the nobility) would kill their fathers. When the whole city was reeling from the arson and slaughter, they would storm out of Rome to link up with Catiline.

During these preparations and rehearsals Cethegus was repeatedly grumbling about the laziness of his comrades. By fussing over plans and postponing the day of attack, he believed they were squandering precious opportunities. In such an hour of peril it was action, not thought, that was needed; and if a few men would help him, he would mount a direct attack on the Curia despite the passivity of the rest. By nature he was wild, violent, and ready for action: he believed that the greatest good lay in speed of movement.

XLIV. But following Cicero's guidance, the Allobroges made contact with the other plotters through Gabinius. They required a sworn oath from Lentulus, Cethegus, Statilius and Cassius; so authenticated, they brought it to the other conspirators. In no other way were they able to be persuaded to take part in the plan. The others revealed no suspicions; Cassius promised that he would come[63] in a short time, and left Rome just before the Allobrogian legates. In order that the Allobroges might strengthen their partnership in goodwill (which had been both given and accepted)

------

[63] I.e., to Gaul.

with Catiline on their return journey home, Lentulus sent with them a man named Titus Volturcius from Crotona. He gave Volturcius a letter[64] for Catiline that contained the words below:

> You will know who I am from the man I have sent to you. Make yourself realize how much danger you are in, and remember that you are a man. Consider closely what your plans call for; seek help from everyone, even from the weakest.

To this he also added a question. Since he had been officially judged an enemy by the senate, on whose advice was he repudiating any help from slaves?[65] In the city, what he ordered had been prepared; he himself should not delay in moving his forces closer.

XLV. Once these preparations had been completed and the appointed night arrived for them to leave, Cicero (who had been advised of everything from the legates) ordered the praetors Lucius Valerius Flaccus and Caius Pomptinus to take the Allobrogian delegation discretely into custody at the Mulvian Bridge. He explained everything to them and extended his thanks; as for the specifics, he allowed them to do what was required by the situation. These men—who were experienced soldiers—positioned their guards without attracting attention just as they had been instructed, and quietly occupied the bridge.

After the legates came to the designated spot with Volturcius, immediately on both sides loud noises arose; the Gauls quickly realized what was happening and gave themselves up to the

---

[64] Roman letters were tied with string. The knots were covered with wax, and this was then impressed with a seal. To open a letter, one would have to cut the string.

[65] Implying that since he had already been declared an outlaw, he might as well accept help from the slave class.

praetors without delay. Volturcius at first urged on his companions and defended himself with his gladius against the greater opposing numbers. Then when the legates abandoned him he called out desperately to Pomptinus (with whom he was on close terms) for his safety; finally, his confidence drained and in fear of losing his life, he surrendered to the praetors as if they were battlefield enemies.

XLVI. After these events had taken place, everything was quickly reported by messengers to the consul. Yet he was filled simultaneously with both joy and deep concern. He was exultant knowing that with the conspiracy exposed the state had been delivered from danger; but he was also apprehensive and uncertain about what action should be taken when so many notable citizens had been implicated in a crime of such magnitude. For while he believed their punishment would be a burden to him, their evasion of punishment would fatally weaken the republic.

After building up his resolve he ordered Lentulus, Cethegus, Statilius, and Gabinius to be summoned before him, as well as a certain Caeparius of Terracina, who was planning to go to Apulia to incite a slave insurrection. The others appeared without delay; but Caeparius, having left his home a short time before, fled the city limits entirely after learning of his indictment. The consul himself escorted Lentulus—who was a praetor—while holding him by the hand; he ordered the rest to come under guard to the Temple of Concord.[66] He called a meeting of the senate in this building with all ranks present in their greatest number; he then led in Volturcius with his legates. He also ordered the praetor Flaccus to bring the satchel of letters he had confiscated from the Gallic envoys.[67]

---

[66] A temple located on the west end of the Roman Forum and dedicated to the goddess Concordia.

[67] The Allobroges. Sallust repeats the word *legatus* (envoy, ambassador,

XLVII. Volturcius was interrogated about his movements, the letters, and eventually about his plan and its ultimate purpose. At first he manufactured a story, denying knowledge of the conspiracy; later, ordered to testify under a grant of immunity,[68] he disclosed all that had happened. He revealed that he had been accepted as an associate of Gabinius and Caeparius only a few days before and knew no more than the legates; but he was used to hearing from Gabinius and Caeparius that Publius Autronius, Servius Sulla, Lucius Vargenteius and many others in addition were also part of the conspiracy.

The Gauls likewise confessed, and the lying Lentulus was silenced not only by his letters but by statements he had been in the habit of making. He had said that three of the Sibylline books[69] predicted the rule of Rome by three men of the Cornelii family; before him were Cinna and Sulla, and he himself was the third, whose destiny it would be to take power in the city. In addition this was the twentieth year since the burning of the Capitol, a year that diviners believed (from the observation of portents) would herald the onset of a bloody civil war. So after the letters had been read and each man acknowledged his personal seal, the senate ordered that once Lentulus had resigned from office he and the others should be held under a personal recognizance bond.[70] Thus Lentulus was delivered to Publius Lentulus Spintheri, who was

---

legate) in this sentence and in the one preceding.

[68] The phrase used here is *fide publica*, which literally is "under the public faith" or "by the public trust." The modern concept of immunity from prosecution fits best as a translation.

[69] The Sibylline books were famous books of prophecy supposedly consulted in times of crisis during the republic and early empire. According to legend they were obtained by the last king of Rome, Tarquinius Superbus.

[70] Modern criminal procedure in the United States has a rough equivalent in a bail hearing at arraignment when a judge releases a defendant on his "own recognizance." No cash equivalent or surety is posted; only the promise of the defendant to appear is required.

serving as aedile; Cethegus was turned over to Quintus Cornificius, Statilius to Caius Caesar, Gabinius to Marcus Crassus, and Caeparius (he had just been returned to custody from his fugitive status) to the senator Gnaeus Terentius.

XLVIII. Meanwhile the lower classes—which at first in their desire for great changes thirsted for war a little too much—experienced a change of heart once the conspiracy had been exposed and condemned the schemes of Catiline; they elevated Cicero up to the heavens, showing as much giddiness and joy as if they had been delivered from servitude. Others thought that acts of war would provide them more in plunder than in detriment; but arson they believed to be cruel, excessive, and the greatest threat, since their personal resources were all they had for daily living and survival.

The next day a man named Lucius Tarquinius was led before the senate. Some said he had been brought back from his journey to link up with Catiline. When he said that he would testify about the conspiracy if given a public grant of immunity, he was ordered by the consul to state what he knew; he then gave the senate almost the same information as that provided by Volturcius with regard to the preparations to set fires, the killing of public figures, and the path of the terrorists.[71] In addition, he said he had been sent by Marcus Crassus as the man to reassure Catiline that the detainment of Lentulus, Cethegus, and other members of the conspiracy should not rattle him; and that he should make haste even more to approach the city, in order the restore the morale of the others, and that they might be rescued more easily from danger.

But when Tarquinius named Crassus, a nobleman of great wealth and supreme political influence, some considered the

---

[71] This is not too strong a word. The phrase here is *de itinere hostium*; or "on the path of the enemies." But the conspirators were engaged in what we would today call terrorism.

testimony unbelievable. Others, however, were of the opinion that it was true: but they argued that in such a moment of crisis a man so powerful should be placated rather than provoked. A good many were also under contractual obligations to Crassus through private business dealings. They angrily insisted that the informant was lying, and proposed that the matter should be referred to the senate.

Thus a full session of the senate decided—on the advice of Cicero—that the disclosures of Tarquinius seemed to be false, and that he should be kept in custody and given no further limelight unless he revealed on whose instruction he had lied about such a material issue. There were some at this time who supposed that this evidence had been fabricated by Publius Autronius, so that by fingering Crassus as entangled in the conspiracy, he could shield the others behind the shadow of Crassus's notoriety. Others said that Tarquinius had been deliberately sent by Cicero in order to prevent Crassus from gaining sympathy for the plotters and—as was his habit—becoming their advocate, which would complicate matters for the republic. Afterwards I heard Crassus himself talking about how this affront was foisted upon him by Cicero.

XLIX. But at the same time Quintus Catulus and Caius Piso were unable to persuade Cicero either by special requests, favors, or rewards to implicate Caius Caesar falsely using the Allobroges or some other doctored evidence. Each of these men nursed the greatest personal enmity for Caesar. Piso's antagonism arose when he was accused of an extrajudicial execution of some person in Transalpine Gaul while on trial for unjust enrichment.[72] Catulus became infected with hate for Caesar when running for the office of pontifex; at an advanced age and having achieved the greatest honors, he was handed an electoral defeat by the very young

---

[72] Extortion or corruption. The phrase used is "in a trial for recovering money" or *in iudicio pecuniarum repetundarum*.

Caesar. Since Catulus was deeply in debt on account of his great generosity in private life and excessive expenditures in public office, accusing Caesar seemed to be the politically expedient thing to do.

But when they were unable to get the consul to concur with the false accusation, they individually began to go around and circulate false rumors that they claimed to have heard from Volturcius or the Allobroges. They incited such ill-feeling against Caesar that a few Roman knights (whether motivated by the seriousness of the crisis or inconstancy of character) who were standing as an armed protection force around the Temple of Concord threatened Caesar with their swords as he was leaving the senate so that they could advertise their devotion to the republic.

L. While these events were happening in the senate, and when the Allobrogian legates and Titus Volturcius had been rewarded when their testimony was confirmed, Lentulus's ex-slaves and a few of his clients took off on their own little mission: they began to incite workmen and servants in the streets to break Lentulus out of custody. For the most part they tried to seek out leaders of mobs who for a price were used to causing trouble for the republic. Moreover, Cethegus through intermediaries was begging his family and some selected, trained freedmen to seize the initiative, form an armed group, and liberate him from confinement.

When the consul became aware of these preparations, he positioned armed guards as the time and situation called for. Summoning the senate, he raised the question regarding what should be done with the men who had been arrested; just before this, however, a full session of the senate had decided that they had committed crimes against the republic. Decimus Junius Silanus, who had been chosen consul at this time, was the first man asked his view on what sentence should be given to those held in confinement as well as what Lucius Cassius, Publius Furius, Publius Umbrenus, and Titus Annius deserved if they might be arrested.

He decided they should be executed. Later, moved by Caius Caesar's speech, he said he would go along with Tiberius Nero's motion when it came to a vote; Nero reckoned the issue should be reconsidered once the security forces were augmented. When his turn in the voting came[73] and Caesar was asked by the consul what the sentence should be, he said the following words:

LI. "Conscript fathers,[74] all men who sit in judgment on uncertain issues ought to be truly free from rancor, favoritism, anger, and sentimentality. The mind cannot easily perceive the truth when these emotions obstruct us; and no man ever obeyed both passion and consideration at the same time. When you concentrate your mind, it produces sound judgment; if passion controls, then the mind is in its grip, and the intellect produces nothing. I should recall many times, conscript fathers, when kings and peoples inflamed by rage or undue compassion decided things badly: but I prefer to talk about how our forefathers acted wisely and considerately without regard for the passions of the mind.

"During the Macedonian war, which we fought with king Perses, the great and distinguished state of the Rhodians—kept afloat by the resources of the Roman people—was ungrateful and disloyal to us. But after the war was concluded and the Rhodians' situation was being debated, our ancestors let them off unpunished, so that no one might say the war's cause was due to a desire for plunder rather than a desire to avenge an injury suffered. The same thing happened during all the Punic wars when the Carthaginians often—both during times of peace and while

---

[73] Questions in the senate were decided by majority vote. This was ascertained either by counting of votes (*numeratio*) or by senators moving to different sides of the chamber (*discessio*). *See* Aulus Gellius XIV.7.

[74] A formal term of address (*patres conscripti*) used for members of the senate during speeches. It was originally intended to acknowledge members of distinguished families (*patres*) and senators who were "newly elected" (*conscripti*).

truces were in effect—committed treacherous actions. The Romans never responded in kind when they had the chance: they asked more what would be consistent with their dignity, rather than asking what the law would allow them to get away with.

"You must be mindful of the same thing, conscript fathers, so that you do not pay more attention to the crimes of Publius Lentulus and the others than you do to your own dignity, and that you do not take more counsel of your anger than of your own good name. Now if a suitable punishment for their actions can be found, I will agree to new discussions. But if the magnitude of the crime exceeds all natural limits, I believe in using the existing remedies imposed by the laws.

"Most of those who expressed their sentiments before me voiced sympathy for the fate of the republic with eloquence and grandeur. They pointed out the cruelty of war and how it crushes the defeated: virgins and young boys raped; children ripped away from the protection of their parents; married women suffering the will of the victors; temples and households plundered; gore and fire in plain sight; and finally weapons, corpses, blood and grief closing in on every side. But by the immortal gods! What would such a speech be made for? Is the purpose to make you outraged against the conspiracy? You think a speech will emotionally fire up a man who has not actually experienced such savagery?

"It is not so. No man considers his own injuries unimportant; and many consider their sufferings more serious than they really are. But freedom, conscript fathers, is being able to choose one thing or another. When those who live lives of obscurity commit some crime through anger, few people ever find out; their reputation and fortune are the same. But for those gifted with great power who hold high positions, the entire world is aware of *their* actions. Thus the least freedom is found in the greatest fortune. One ought to feel anger very little, and neither covet nor hate. What is anger for the common man is considered arrogance and cruelty when seen in a leader.

"As for me, I truly believe that every torture is not enough to compensate for the crimes of these accused men. But the majority of mortal men remembers only the most recent things; and in the case of bad men, it forgets their evil deeds and gossips about their punishment, if it were especially severe. I know for a fact that Decimus Silanus—a vigorous and powerful character—said what he said out of devotion to the republic, and that at the critical moment he made use of neither favoritism nor partiality. So have I known the personal style and discipline of this man.

"In fact his opinion seems to me not cruel—for what really could be cruel for such men!—but instead alien to the traditions of our country. For surely either fear or the possibility of injury forced you, Silanus, to decide on a new kind of punishment when you were a consul-elect. It is unnecessary to speak about fear, especially since—thanks to the consul's diligence—the best men are serving as guards under arms. I can indeed speak about punishment, and believe this to be true: when grief and suffering dominate, death is not a punishment but a deliverance from mortal cares. It erases all mortal misery; beyond it neither worry nor joys exist.

"But by the immortal gods, why didn't you offer the suggestion that they be flogged? Was it because the Porcian law prevented it?[75] But other laws permit that, once a citizen is condemned, he may be exiled rather than put to death. Or was it because it is more serious to be whipped than to be killed? What is considered devastating or too serious for men convicted of such a crime? If it was because whipping is too lenient, why does it make sense to adhere to the letter of the law on a minor issue, when you have already neglected the spirit of the law in a major

---

[75] A series of three laws passed (along with the Valerian laws) between 199 and 185 B.C. that abolished cruel and unusual forms of punishment for Roman citizens, such as flogging and crucifixion.

one?[76] Who indeed will find fault with a decree passed against those who would destroy the republic?

"Circumstance, time, and the whim of Fortune direct all nations. Whatever happens to the defendants here will be justified; but consider, conscript fathers, the precedent of your decision for other cases. Every bad precedent first came from good cases. But when official power is wielded by incompetents or men who are less than good, this new precedent is transferred from those who are worthy and suitable to those who are unworthy and unsuitable.[77]

"Once they had defeated the Athenians, the Spartans set up thirty men to manage the affairs of the Athenian republic.[78] These men at first began by summarily executing the very worst and most hated men in the city. The population was quite happy and said it had been well done. But little by little permissiveness increased, so that both good men and bad equally could be killed at the pleasure of the junta; and the rest were kept in the grip of fear. In this way civil society was brutalized: it paid a very high price for its irresponsible happiness.[79] In our own memory, when the victor Sulla ordered to be slain Damasippus and others of his type who had risen to prominence in the republic through evil, who did not praise this order? Everyone said that these criminal rogues and divisive factionalists, who had tormented the republic with their schemes, were deservedly put to death.

---

[76] The Porcian laws protected Roman citizens from floggings and summary executions. Silanus had suggested the conspirators be executed without trial, yet had (according to Caesar) been squeamish about flogging them. Caesar is criticizing the apparent inconsistency between pushing for execution while shying away from lesser prohibited punishments.

[77] I.e., unworthy and unsuitable for the punishment dictated by prior precedent.

[78] This passage about the "Thirty Tyrants" refers to events that happened in Athens at the end of the Peloponnesian War in 404 B.C.

[79] The happiness it expressed when the junta first started killing "bad" men.

"But this was the beginning of a great catastrophe. For now when someone wanted another's house or country villa—or even eventually his home furnishings or clothing—he would make efforts to add that man's name to the proscription list.[80] Those for whom the death of Damasippus had been a celebration were themselves marched off to the executioner before long; the purge did not end until Sulla had satiated all his people with the confiscated property of the victims. I fear none of these things for our own times or from Marcus Tullius, but in a large nation there are many different types of characters. It may happen that at another time, and with another consul who has control over the army, some opportunistic lie may be believed as truth. When the consul then draws out his *gladius*—with this precedent in effect and with the endorsement of the senate—who will set a boundary for him or try to control him?[81]

"Our ancestors, conscript fathers, were never lacking in prudence or audacity. Pride never prevented them from imitating foreign institutions as long as they were sound. From the Samnites they took their armor and weapons of war, and mostly from the Etruscans did they adopt the symbols of civil office. Eventually whenever something suitable was encountered from friendly nation or foe, they embraced it at home with the greatest enthusiasm: they preferred to learn from those who were successful rather than be jealous of them. But at the same time— imitating the custom of the Greeks—they adopted the punishment of flogging for citizens as well as the death penalty for those judged guilty.

"Later the republic matured, and factions of citizens grew along with the population; the innocent began to be maltreated

---

[80] Proscription was the term used to describe extrajudicial executions by the ruling party. Lists were drawn up for those who could legally be killed.
[81] The *gladius* was the short Roman sword. The image of the consul drawing his sword is of course a metaphor for using force.

and other injustices took place. So the Porcian law and other statutes of this kind were prepared, in which the condemned were legally given the option of exile. I believe, conscript fathers, that this is a compelling reason why we should not quite take on a new policy. Certainly the masculine virtue and wisdom of our ancestors—who created this empire with few resources—was superior to ours, seeing that we can hardly preserve what we inherited. Is it right for them[82] to be sent away to augment Catiline's army? Absolutely not. I believe their assets should be forfeited to the state; that they be kept in custody in the municipalities having the most suitable resources; and that no one bring any of their cases before the senate nor attempt a public referendum. Should anyone try otherwise, the senate should consider him as acting against the state and public security."

LII. After Caesar concluded his speech, other senators agreed to this or that from the various solutions put forward. But when Marcius Porcius Cato was asked for his position, he spoke in this way:

"Conscript fathers, when I think about the conspiracy and the danger we have lived with, and when I weigh carefully the opinions of a good number of us here, I find myself of a much different mind.[83] My colleagues seem preoccupied with the punishment of these defendants who have taken steps to wage war against their country, parents, altars, and homes. But the situation warns us to protect ourselves from them rather than to debate what we should do with them under the legal codes. Where other types of crimes have been committed, you could handle the situation in this way; but in this case, unless you take steps to ensure the crime does not happen, you invoke the law in vain once the deed is done. When a city is captured, there is nothing left for the conquered.

---

[82] The prisoners in custody.

[83] Different from Caesar's opinion.

"But by the immortal gods, I reach out to you who have cherished your houses, country estates, statues, and paintings more than the republic. If you wish by whatever means to keep these things that you have your arms wrapped around; if you want to have the leisure time for enjoying your luxuries, wake up and take charge of the country. This is not a matter about taxes or about bad things our allies have done: our freedom and our lives are at stake! Very often, conscript fathers, have I spoken at length before this assembly; often I have complained about the luxury and avarice of our fellow-citizens. And for this reason I have many enemies among my fellows. I, who never gave myself or my soul any credit for their sins, did not easily forgive the bad acts of someone else's impulses. But although you gave my opinion little weight, the republic nevertheless stayed strong: opulence endured negligence.

"Now, however, the issue in play is not whether we are living under good or bad morals, nor how big or magnificent the empire of the Roman people is, but this: whether everything we have or that is connected to us will become the property of the enemy. Here I see that someone suggests clemency and compassion. Yet for a while now we have indeed lost the true names for things. It was because carelessness in giving away other people's goods was called "generosity," and recklessness in doing evil things was called "courage," that the republic is now in such dire straits. Since these are the habits of our era, then let such people be cavalier with the security of our allies; let them be compassionate with those who rob the treasury! But let them not be wasteful with our own blood and, by sparing a few criminals, send all good men to oblivion.

"A short time ago Caius Caesar spoke agreeably and with polish in this chamber about life and death, taking (I assume) as fairy-tales those things we are told about the Underworld, where the good and the bad have separate paths and the bad end up in the region that is foul, rough, loathsome, ghastly, and dangerous.

So he reckoned that their property should be confiscated, and that they be remanded to custody in municipalities under Roman jurisdiction; fearing, evidently, that if they stayed in Rome they might be broken out of prison either by other conspirators or by some mob. As if there were bad men and criminals only in Rome and not everywhere in Italy, or as if criminal daring was not most likely in just those places where the ability to resist it was the most feeble!

"This truly is why this proposal[84] is ineffective if he fears additional dangers from the conspirators. But if he alone has no fear when everyone else does, then this is all the more reason why you and I should be afraid. Know that when you render judgment on Publius Lentulus and his accomplices, you will for certain be ruling on the fate of Catiline's army and the other members of the conspiracy. The more decisively you do this, the more you will undermine the enemy's morale; but if they see you dither in the slightest way, they will come at us with the utmost ferocity. Don't believe that our ancestors made our republic great from very little just by force of arms. If this were true, we would have a much more wondrous society than they did, since we have more allies and citizens, as well as more weapons and horses, than they ever had. There were other things they had that made them great, things that are lacking in us: a hardworking ethic at home, just power abroad, and a free spirit in public debate that was marked by neither sin nor passion.

"In place of these qualities we now have luxury and greed, public poverty, and extreme private wealth. We praise riches, and we follow indolence. There is no separation made between good and bad, and ambition seizes all the rewards of virtue. This is no surprise. Where each of you is preoccupied with his own individual interest, where you fixate on pleasures at home and

---

[84] Caesar's earlier proposal.

serve the agenda of money and popularity here, it inevitably happens that an attack takes place on a republic that is a shell of its former self.

"But I set this aside. Upper-class citizens have conspired to burn Rome. They have brought in the Gauls—sworn enemies of the Roman people—to wage their war. The leader of the enemy with his army hovers over our heads. Do you now hesitate and even doubt what you should do with captured enemies inside the city walls? I suppose you may have mercy on them; they are young men led down the wrong path by ambition. So then release them with their arms! If they were then to take up arms against the state, this clemency and compassion of yours would come right back to you as suffering. Of course the situation is drastic: but you do not fear this.

"Yet you do indeed fear it! You procrastinate through laziness and an absence of backbone, waiting for either this or that and blissfully relying on divine intervention, something that has often saved this republic in its greatest hours of danger. The help of the gods is not obtained by prayers or by effeminate groveling before the altar: things turn out successfully because of vigilance, fast action, and wise counsel. When you surrender to inaction and idleness, you ask for divine help in vain: the gods are angry and hostile.

"Among our ancestors, Aulus Manlius Torquatus ordered his own son to be executed during one of the Gallic wars when he engaged the enemy in combat in violation of orders. The brave youth paid the ultimate price for his excess of courage. Do you now dither about what to do with these most ruthless of traitors? No doubt their past lives stand in stark contrast to their present crime. Show mercy on the honor of Lentulus, if he ever spared his own modesty, reputation, or any anyone else for that matter, whether god or man. Pardon the youth Cethegus, unless he has committed violence against his country a second time. But what should I say about Gabinius, Statilius, and Caeparius? If any of them had ever had a useful thought, they would not have joined this conspiracy against the republic.

"By Hercules![85] Conscript fathers, if there were ever a situation for a mistake, I would easily prefer you to be corrected, since you give my words little thought.[86] But we are hard-pressed on all sides. Catiline is squeezing our throats with his army. Other enemies are inside our walls and in the very heart of the city. Neither can anyone prepare or draw up plans secretly: what is most important is that we must hurry. Therefore I recommend the following. Since our republic has come under the greatest danger from this evil plot of some criminal citizens; and since their culpability has been shown by the evidence of Titus Volturcius and the Allobrogian envoys, and they have admitted to planning assassination, arson, and other terrible and savage acts against their fellow-citizens and country; I say that *those who have confessed must be viewed as caught in the very act of committing capital crimes, and deserving of the punishment of our ancestors.*"[87]

LIII. After Cato sat down, the ex-consuls as well as a majority of the senate praised his sentiments and made a great show of his strength of character; some chided others, calling them timid. Cato stood out as great and especially perceptive, and the decision of the senate passed just as he had advised.

But for me, as I had read and heard a great deal about the impressive deeds of the Roman people at home and in the arena of conflict on both land and sea, I eventually became consumed with a desire to understand what special Roman quality was able

---

[85] This was a common exclamatory oath to express surprise or amazement.
[86] Meaning "if we had the time for you to be proven wrong by external events, that would be the best way to teach you the error of your ways."
[87] Cato clearly wants the conspirators executed. By describing them as having been caught red-handed in capital crimes (*de manufestis rerum capitalium*), he leaves little room for doubt.

to produce such achievements. I was aware that they had often contended with large numbers of enemy forces with only a small number of men; I knew that with few resources they had waged great wars with rich kings, and in these contests had often endured the cruelty of Fortune; and I understood that the Greeks surpassed the Romans in eloquence, while the Gauls exceeded them in renown for war. After much consideration, it was clear that all of this had come about as a result of the outstanding virtue of a small number of citizens: and it was due to this fact that humility overcame opulence, and a small elite asserted itself over the multitude. But after society was corrupted by soft living and inactivity, the state in its turn was able to tolerate by its own greatness the defects of its civil officials and generals and, just like an exhausted parent,[88] Rome produced no one who had great character for a long period of time.

But in my own time there have been two men of unsurpassed character with quite different personalities: Marcus Cato and Caius Caesar. Because the opportunity is before us, it is not my wish to allow it to slip away in silence. I shall thus discuss, to the best of my ability, the nature and character of each of these men.

LIV. They were comparable to each other in family origins, age, and eloquence; in greatness of soul, they were about the same; and they enjoyed equal renown, despite achieving it in different ways. Caesar derived his greatness from his generosity and public service, and Cato from his personal integrity. One man fashioned great deeds through clemency and compassion, while the strictness of the other brought him public honor. Caesar achieved renown by giving, helping, and forgiving, and Cato by never participating in bribery. One was a refuge for the downtrodden, the other a curse for the corrupt. One was praised for his good nature, the other for his steadfastness.

---

[88] The analogy refers to a mother no longer able to produce offspring.

Caesar had trained his spirit to work hard and sleep little; to neglect his own purposes for the goals of his friends, and to deny them nothing that deserved to be given. He wished for supreme authority, an army, and a new war where his masculine virtue might shine forth. But Cato was devoted to modesty, decorum, and most importantly moral strictness. He neither competed with the rich in wealth nor with the partisans in partisanship, but with the robust in virtue, with the restrained in modesty, and with the disciplined in self-control. He preferred to *be* a good man rather than be seen as one; hence the less he sought renown, the more it followed him.

LV. After the senate consented to the views of Cato, as I have described, the consul believed a prudent measure would be to wait for a night to see if some new development intervened. He also ordered the triumvirs to make ready the execution he had proposed; and after putting guards in place, he transported Lentulus to prison. He had the praetors do the same thing for the other defendants. Once you enter the prison, there is an area about twelve feet below ground level called the Tullianum that is found when you ascend a little towards the left. This is buttressed on all sides by walls, and above it is a room covered with a sturdy stone roof; its presence—derived from its lack of maintenance, its darkness, and its foul odors—is ghastly and sinister. After Lentulus had been cast down into this dungeon, the executioners carried out the capital sentence as instructed by throttling him to death.[89] Thus this patrician from the renowned Cornelii family— who had once occupied the seat of consular power in Rome— made his departure from life in a way that was worthy of his character and actions. The same method of execution was meted out to Cethegus, Statilius, Gabinius, and Caeparius.

---

[89] Literally "crushing his neck by strangulation" (*laqueo gulam fregere*).

LVI. While these events were happening in Rome, Catiline formed two legions by adding Manlius's forces to the existing units he already possessed. He filled his cohorts[90] as far as the number of available men allowed. Finally, as each volunteer and fellow conspirator arrived in camp, he distributed them equally in the ranks; in a short time the legions were enrolled with a sufficient number of men, whereas in the beginning he could not field more than two thousand. But out of the entire force only about a quarter were equipped with traditional military arms; the remainder outfitted themselves with whatever weapons they could scrounge, such as javelins and long spears. Some even carried sharpened stakes.

When Antonius approached with his army, Catiline set a line of march through the mountains. He moved his camp first in the direction of the city and then towards Gaul, not giving the enemy the chance to engage him. He hoped that within a day he would be able to augment his forces with significant numbers if his allies in Rome could carry out their scheme. In the meantime he turned away slaves who were initially drawn to him in great numbers. Relying on the existing resources of the conspiracy, he considered it to be at odds with his purposes to share a citizens' cause with fugitive slaves.[91]

LVII. But after a messenger arrived in camp with news that the conspiracy had been exposed in Rome, and that Lentulus, Cethegus, and the others I have described above had been executed, a great many men who had been enticed to war by the hope of plunder or revolution melted away. Catiline led the

---

[90] In Sallust's time a cohort contained about 500 men, and a legion was composed of 10 cohorts. Sallust claims that Catiline was able to field two full legions.

[91] Catiline well knew that arming slaves might fatally alienate Roman public opinion against him. Such a move would be seen as a direct attack on the social order, not just an attempt to seize power.

remainder on long marches through harsh terrain to the region of Pistoria; his plan was to escape to Transalpine Gaul on little-used footpaths. But Quintus Metellus Celer was stationed in the Picene region with three legions, and he judged that Catiline would do the very same thing we have just described as a consequence of his untenable situation. Thus when he learned of Catiline's escape route from deserters, he quickly moved his camp and placed himself at the base of the same mountains that Catiline would have to descend during his dash into Gaul.

Antonius was not far away either; he was tracking the fugitives with a large army over more level terrain.[92] Once he saw that he was trapped between the mountains and the enemy units, that the tide had turned against him in Rome, and that he could hope neither for escape nor assistance, Catiline decided to engage Antonius in battle, calculating that the best course of action in the situation was to let fate decide the outcome in battle. He therefore summoned his men for a meeting and delivered the following speech.

LVIII. "Soldiers, of course I know that words alone do not give martial virtue, nor does an army transform from soft to hard or from timid to daring by their commander's speech. Whatever amount of audacity each man possesses through his own personality or habits is what is usually displayed in combat. It is useless to encourage someone who is not stirred to action by glory or risks: the soul's fear blocks the ears. But I have called you here to offer a bit of advice, and to explain the reason behind my course of action.

"You know, soldiers, all about the magnitude of the disaster that Lentulus brought on himself and us by his procrastination and

---

[92] The text here possibly has an interpolation. The manuscripts have the word *expedito* or *expeditus* in the sentence (*Neque tamen Antonius procul aberat, utpote qui magno exercitu locis aequioribus expedito in fuga sequeretur*). But the word seems unnecessary.

incompetence. I could not move into Gaul while I waited for help to come from Rome.[93] Just as I do, of course, you now understand everything about where our situation stands. Two enemy armies are opposing us: one in the direction of Rome, and the other towards Gaul. The lack of grain and other supplies prevents us from staying much longer in this location, even if we may very much want to. Wherever we choose to go, the way must be opened with the sword.[94] For this reason I remind you to be firm and adopt a mission-oriented spirit. When you enter battle remember that you carry riches, distinction, glory, and even liberty and your native country in your right hands. If we conquer, we will all be safe; provisions in great quantity, as well as towns and colonies, will be open before us. But if we allow fear to take hold of us, all these things will be reversed: no place and no friend will protect the man who is unable to defend himself with arms. Besides, soldiers, different motivations cast shadows over us and them: we fight for our country, liberty, and for our lives; their fight is an empty quest to maintain the power of the elites. You should attack more aggressively, and remember your uncompromised virtue.

"You might have lived out your years in exile in total disgrace. At Rome a few of you could have waited for others' handouts after losing all your own property. But because these options were seen as repellent and intolerable for real men, you chose this present path. If you want to leave this behind, you need audacity: no one except the winner replaces war with peace. To hope for safety in retreat at a time when you have turned away from the enemy the weapons that protect you: this truly is insane! The greatest dangers in battle always fall on those who are the most fearful. Audacity acts as a solid protective wall.[95]

---

[93] Meaning that he was waiting for Lentulus to succeed in Rome and send reinforcements.

[94] *Quocumque ire placet, ferro iter aperiundum est.* Compare this to the quote by Virgil in *Aen.* II.494: *Fit via vi,* "the road comes through force."

[95] Meaning that audacity functions like a barrier to keep out fear (*audacia pro muro habetur*).

"When I think about you, soldiers, and remember the things you have accomplished, I hold a strong expectation of victory. Your spirit, youth, and courage inspire me; and besides this is necessity, which makes even the fearful brave. The narrow passages of this place prevent the enemy force from being able to surround us. But if fortune refuses to acknowledge your courage, be sure not to leave this life unavenged. Do not be taken and slaughtered like cattle: go down fighting like real men, and make the enemy earn a bloody and bitter victory."

LIX. When he finished speaking he lingered for a few moments and then ordered the battle-standards to sound,[96] then led his drawn-up formations down to level ground. After removing all the horses (which would amplify the soldiers' fighting spirit by evenly distributing the danger) and going on foot himself, he arranged his army as the terrain and his units required. Now because this level ground was bordered on the left by mountains and on the right by coarse, rocky terrain, he placed eight cohorts in the front and held back the rest of the units in tighter formation as a reserve.[97] From these he placed in the front rank both the centurions (all hand-picked and seasoned veterans) and the most well-armed of the common soldiers. He ordered Caius Manlius to command the right flank, and a man from Faesulae to take charge of the left. Catiline placed himself beside the eagle, which Caius Marius was said to have had during the

---

[96] Presumably by having the *cornicen* (the military horn-blower) sound off. The job of the *cornicen* was to sound orders to Roman military units. He did this with a large curved horn (*cornu*) and marched with the standard-bearer (*signifer,* derived from *signum ferens*, or "bearing the standard").
[97] A cohort formally contained six centuries (*centuriae*) of 80 men each (480 men total). Since a standard legion was composed of 5000 men, we can say that a cohort was about one-tenth of a legion.

Cimbrian War, along with his freedmen and servants.[98]

On the other side Caius Antonius (who could not participate in the battle due to an illness that made him unable to walk[99]) relinquished command of his army to his executive officer Marcus Petreius. Petreius put the veteran cohorts he had drafted to deal with the rebellion in front; behind these he placed the rest of the army in reserve. Circling his troops while mounted on horseback, he called out to each of them by name, inspiring them to action; he asked every man to remember that he was fighting to protect his country, children, places of worship, and households against poorly-equipped bandits. A seasoned military man who had served in the army with distinction for over thirty years as tribune, prefect, lieutenant or praetor, he knew most of his men and their great achievements personally. By talking about these things, he lit up the soldiers' spirits.

LX. After making his preparations, Petreius gave a signal with the trumpet and ordered the cohorts to advance little by little. The enemy army did the same. Once things had reached a point where the *ferentarii*[100] could be committed to the fighting, the two opposing forces ran and clashed each other with great noise; they dropped their long pikes and pulled out their short swords. Petreius's veterans, remembering their old courage, pressed the enemy hard in fierce combat at close quarters; the other side stood their ground without flinching, and the battle was joined with

---

[98] The "eagle" was the Roman battle-standard. The Cimbrian War (113-101 B.C.) was waged between the Roman republic and two Germanic tribes. Marius's leadership was decisive in securing victory.

[99] The phrase used here is *pedibus aeger*, which some translators have interpreted as a reference to gout.

[100] The term *ferentarius* refers to a lightly-armed Roman soldier carrying missile weapons only (i.e., javelins) and kept on the wings of a military unit for support.

brutal violence. Meanwhile Catiline was busy with his light infantry in the very front line. He aided those who were exhausted, fetched replacements for the wounded, and took care of every battle contingency. He even joined in the fighting himself, not infrequently striking down an opponent; he thus carried out the duties of a courageous soldier and a good field commander at the same time.

When Petreius—contrary to what he had expected—saw that Catiline was putting up such a strong fight, he led his praetorian cohort[101] into the center of the enemy's line. This shattered their cohesion, and he killed the remnants still offering resisting in other parts of the battle-line. Finally he struck at Catiline's force on both sides at once. Manlius and the above-mentioned man from Faesulae were among the first to fall. Once Catiline saw that his army was cut to pieces and that he was left with only a few men, he flung himself into action where the enemy was most densely packed, and was there mortally wounded while fighting.

LXI. When the battle had finished, you could truly see how much audacity, and what force of spirit, there had been in Catiline's army. For practically every man covered with his inert body—when he breathed his last breath—the spot on which he fought so bravely while alive. A few in the center who had been crushed by the praetorian cohort lay some distance from the rest, but all of these had wounds that were directly facing the enemy.[102] Catiline indeed was found far from his own men among some corpses of the enemy, still breathing, and preserving in his facial expression that ferocity of spirit he showed in life. Out of his entire rebel army not a single free-born citizen had been captured either during the battle or while in flight; his men had placed no

---

[101] As noted above the praetorian cohort was an elite force of handpicked men.

[102] Meaning that they did not turn and flee from the enemy.

greater value on their own lives than on the lives of their enemies.[103]

But the army of the Roman people obtained neither joy nor a bloodless victory. The best men had all either died in combat or had survived it severely wounded. Many who left camp to visit the scene of the fighting or to take what they could from the battlefield discovered, upon turning over the bodies of the enemy, either a friend, an acquaintance, or a family member. There were some who even recognized their personal enemies. Thus in different ways was the entire army moved by exultation and mourning, satisfaction and sorrow.

---

[103] Literally, "they held their own lives and those of the enemy to be of equal weight." (*Ita cuncti suae hostiumque vitae iuxta perpercerant*).

VII. TRANSLATOR'S POSTSCRIPT

So ended the life of Catiline. The number of dead in the Battle of Pistoria is estimated at about three thousand. This historian Dio Cassius (XXXVII.40—41) says that Caius Antonius ordered Catiline to be decapitated and his head sent to Rome as a trophy. Various alleged participants in the plot were rounded up in different parts of Italy, but many of these were acquitted of wrongdoing. Fragments of Catiline's army under a minor conspirator named Lucius Sergius held out and continued to resist in northern Italy for some time after this; but they too were eventually destroyed. In Rome Cicero was showered with accolades by a grateful public for his handling of the crisis. But even this glory would prove to be fleeting.

THE WAR OF JUGURTHA

VIII. Chronology Of Major Events Of The Jugurthine War

Year (B.C.)	Consuls	Major Events
208	M. Claudius, Marcellus, T. Quintius Crispinus	Masinissa becomes king.
203	Cn. Servilius Caepio, C. Servilius Nepos	Masinissa unites Numidia under his rule.
158	Q. Fulvius Nobilior, T. Annius Lusus	Jugurtha born (?).
148	Sp. Postumius Albinus, L. Calpurnius Piso	Masinissa dies and Micipsa becomes king.
140	C. Laelius Sapiens, Q. Servilius Caepio	Marius and Jugurtha serve together under Scipio in the siege of Numantia.
121	Q. Fabius Aemilianus Maximus, L. Opimius	Jugurtha is adopted by Micipsa.
118	M. Porcius Cato, Q. Marcius Rex	Micipsa dies, leaving his sons to succeed him.
117	L. Caecilius Metellus, Q. Mucius Scaevola	Jugurtha murders Hiempsal; Adherbal flees to the Romans.
116	C. Licinius Geta, Q. Fabius Eburnus	Adherbal and Jugurtha's envoys both ask for Roman help.
114	M. Acilius Balbus, C. Porcius Cato	Jugurtha and Adherbal begin fighting again.
113	C. Caecilius Metellus, Cn. Papirius Carbo	Adherbal is defeated and flees to Cirta.

112	M. Livius Drusus, L. Calpurnius Piso	Adherbal sends a letter to the senate. Cirta falls and Adherbal is executed. Romans declare war on Jugurtha
111	P. Cornelius Scipio Nasica, L. Calpurnius Piso Bestia	Calpurnius assigned command of army of Numidia. Jugurtha convinces him to make peace.
110	M. Minucius Rufus, Sp. Postumius Albinus	Jugurtha has Bomilcar kill Massiva at Rome. Albinus leaves his brother Aulus in command of army in Numidia.
109	Q. Caecilius Metellus Numidicus, M. Junius Silanus	Aulus surrenders to Jugurtha at Suthul. Albinus turns over army command to Metellus. Fall of Vacca. Metellus puts Zama to siege.
108	S. Sulpitius Galba, M. Aemilius Scaurus Hortensius	Jugurtha makes and breaks a treaty with Metellus. Thala is captured. Jugurtha makes alliance with Mauretanian king Bocchus.
107	L. Cassius Longinus, C. Marius	Marius given command of Numidian army. He arrives in Africa and takes Capsa.
106	C. Attilius Serranus, Q. Servilius Caepio	Sulla arrives on the scene. Bocchus and Jugurtha are routed near Cirta. Bocchus sends out peace feelers to the Romans.

105	P. Rutilius Rufus, C. Manlius Maximus	Bocchus sends envoys to Marius and then Rome. Bocchus betrays Jugurtha and delivers him to the Romans.

IX. TOPICAL ORGANIZATION OF *THE WAR OF JUGURTHA*

TEXT SECTION(S)	TOPIC(S)
I-III	Importance of good character. Need to control the baser appetites. The mind governs the body. Futility of ruling by force.
IV-VI	Why Sallust left public office. Why the writing of history is important. The lineage of Jugurtha. Jugurtha grows in power. Micipsa becomes nervous.
VII-IX	Jugurtha's great qualities during the siege of Numantia. Scipio advises him to cultivate the Roman people and shun bribes.
X-XII	Micipsa's last words and instructions. Meeting of the three princes. Bad faith of Hiempsal. Murder of Hiempsal by ambush.
XIII-XV	Jugurtha sends envoys to Rome. Reception of the envoys. Adherbal addresses the senate.
XVI-XVIII	Division of Numidia. Who receives what part of the country. The basic geography of northern Africa. The early inhabitants of Africa.
XIX-XXI	Phoenicia, Numidia, and the Moors. Jugurtha attacks Adherbal and war breaks out. Adherbal is cornered; Rome tries to mediate.

XXII-XXIV	Roman envoys arrive in Africa.
	Jugurtha states his position to them.
	He tries to take Cirta.
	Adherbal sends envoys to Rome.
	Adherbal's letter read to the senate
XXV-XXVII	Indecision of the senate.
	Envoys are sent to Africa.
	The mission ends in failure.
	Cirta surrenders; Adherbal is executed.
	Senate raises army and sends it to Africa.
XXVIII-XXX	Calpurnius attacks Numidian towns.
	Jugurtha plans to bribe his way out.
	Hostilities are halted.
	Outrage in Rome at the way peace was made.
XXXI-XXXIII	Memmius's speech to the people.
	The praetor Cassius approaches Jugurtha with an offer.
	Memmius calls a meeting with Jugurtha present.
XXXIV-XXXVI	Jugurtha evades testifying by bribing Baebius.
	Bomilcar murders Massiva, is caught, and confesses.
	Jugurtha leaves Rome and adopts guerrilla tactics.
	Albinus sails for Rome and leaves brother in charge.
XXXVII-XXXIX	Aulus prepares to attack Suthul.
	Aulus is defeated and accepts Jugurtha's terms.
	Albinus decides not to attack at once.
XL-XLII	C. Mamilius Limetanus proposes a bill to indict Jugurtha's collaborators; this passes.
	Origins of civil strife in Rome.
	Why the Gracchi failed.
XLIII-XLV	Metellus prepares for war and leaves for Africa.
	The poor readiness of his army.
	Metellus restores his army's discipline.
XLVI-XLVIII	Metellus moves carefully into Numidia.
	He stations a garrison at Vaga and receives more envoys.
	Jugurtha decides to risk a battle.
XLIX-LI	Metellus spots the enemy and prepares to engage.
	The battle is joined in chaotic fashion.
	Outcome of the battle is unclear.

LII-LIV	The battle continues.
	Link-up of forces and the battle's end.
	The start of guerilla war and counterinsurgency tactics.
LV-LVII	Jugurtha continues to harass the Romans.
	The battle at Sicca; Marius saves the day.
	Battle at Zama begins.
LVIII-LX	Jugurtha attacks the Roman camp. The battle rages.
	Jugurtha tries an ambush. He uses combined arms tactics.
	Siege of the town continues.
LXI-LXIII	Metellus tries to manipulate Bomilcar.
	Jugurtha is talked into surrender but then reverses himself.
	Character of Caius Marius.
LXIV-LXVI	Marius aims for the consulship but Metellus put him off.
	Gauda is approached by Marius.
	The Vagans agree to help Jugurtha.
LXVII-LXIX	The revolt at Vaga.
	Metellus sets out to avenge the massacre.
	Vaga is attacked and plundered.
LXX-LXXII	Bomilcar recruits Nabdalsa in a plot against Jugurtha.
	Nabdalsa's letter is betrayed.
	Nabdalsa declares his innocence to Jugurtha.
	Jugurtha is tormented by fear.
LXXIII-LXXV	Marius wins the consulship.
	Jugurtha and Metellus clash in battle.
	Metellus crosses a vast expanse to reach Thala.
LXXVI-LXXVIII	The fall of Thala.
	The Lepcitani ask Metellus for aid.
	Origin and geography of Lepcis.
LXXIX-LXXXI	The story of the Philaeni brothers.
	Jugurtha convinces King Bocchus to join the war.
	The two kings head for Cirta.
LXXXII-LXXXIV	Metellus hears that Numidia is reassigned to Marius.
	Metellus warns Bocchus not to get involved.
	In Rome Marius makes preparations for war.

X. TEXT OF *THE WAR OF JURGURTHA*

I. In vain does man lament his nature over the fact that it is fragile and impermanent and governed more by chance than by virtue. Deeper inquiry shows, however, that you will find nothing greater or more surpassing, and that human nature more often lacks perseverance than physical strength or an extended age. But the mind is the leader and commander of the life of mortals. He who marches to glory by the path of virtue has an abundance of strength, power, and renown; he does not need fortune, since fortune can neither bestow nor revoke from someone honesty, industry, or any of the other noble qualities. The man consumed by perverse appetites surrenders himself to inertia and the basest cravings of the body. For a short time he enjoys his destructive lusts, where strength, opportunity, and good character are drained away through self-indulgence. Blame is fixed on the "infirmity of human nature," and the engineers of the crime transfer responsibility to some external factor. But if men had the same care for doing good works as they have enthusiasm for chasing what is of no advantage to them—in many cases what is even dangerous and harmful to them—they would more often *rule* fortune than *be ruled* by it, and would advance to such greatness that through their glory they would become immortal among men.

II. For as a human being is composed of both a physical form and a soul, all of our earthly pursuits attend to the nature of either the body or the soul. Thus a beautiful body, great riches, physical strength, and all other attributes of this type melt away in a short time; but surpassing deeds of character are, like the soul, eternal. Ultimately the goods of the body and of fortune have both an inception and a conclusion. Everything that has risen falls, and all that is created grows old. But the soul is imperishable, eternal, and the pilot of mankind; it moves and comprehends all things, but is not itself moved.[104] How we must be shocked, then, at the depravity of those who, devoted to the joys of the body, fritter away their years in luxury and inactivity, as well as those others who allow their personal character—which is greater and more vital than anything else in human nature—to decay from lack of cultivation and an absence of challenges: especially since there are so many and such a wide variety of mental disciplines in which the greatest acclaim may be achieved.

III. Indeed civil and high-ranking military positions—and ultimately all public offices—seem to me very undesirable in our era.[105] Virtue is not rewarded with respect, and those who have gained the appearance of virtue through fraud are neither safe nor more honest as a result. For without doubt to rule a country or a people by force, although you can (and do) fix their problems, is nevertheless monstrous, particularly when all such forced changes foretell killing, exile, and other kinds of violence. It is completely insane to exert oneself futilely to achieve nothing but hatred, unless one holds a destructive and dishonest desire to surrender one's personal integrity and freedom for the power of a small minority.[106]

IV. From among those activities that cultivate the intellect, the most useful is the writing of historical events. Because many have already spoken on its intrinsic worth, I believe I should pass over

---

[104] This passage has a strong Platonic flavor. *See* Cicero's essay "The Dream of Scipio" included in my translation of his *Stoic Paradoxes* (Charleston: Fortress of the Mind Publications, 2015).

[105] Rome was undergoing a time of political upheaval when Sallust was writing. It did not fully end until the establishment of the imperial system.

[106] Presumably referring to the ambitious political figures of his day such as Pompey.

this issue lest someone think that I am egotistically propping up my own avocation with praise. I imagine also that, since I have chosen to spend my remaining years away from public office, there are those who would consider my useful labor to fall under the category of "inactivity." This is certainly true for people who consider the height of productivity to be hobnobbing with the riff-raff and chasing favor at official dinners. But if these same people reflect on the times during which I came into public office, and what kind of men were unable to obtain the same positions (and later what type of men would come to fill the senate), they will certainly appreciate the fact that I changed my mind for valid reasons and not out of laziness, and that greater benefit will come to the country from my "inactivity" than from the public posturings of others.

I have often heard that Quintus Maximus, Publius Scipio, and other distinguished men of our nation would say frequently that, when they looked upon the images of their ancestors, their souls were passionately set ablaze in the quest for virtue.[107] Of course they did not mean that the wax or the image had some sort of power over them, but that the memory of great deeds kindles this flame in the breasts of exceptional men, and that this fire cannot be extinguished until they have brought their own fame and glory to the level of masculine virtue of their exemplars.

But in reality—with today's prevailing moral standards—who does not prefer to compete with our ancestors' riches and luxuries, rather than with their moral rectitude and work ethic? Even the "new men,"[108] who in the past were in the habit of outclassing the nobles with their moral fiber, gradually came to rely more on

---

[107] Looking at "images" meant funeral masks, statues, or busts. Aristocratic Romans sometimes displayed wax busts of their ancestors in their homes. *See* Pliny, *Hist. Nat.* XXXV.2.

[108] This term (*novus homo*) was used to denote a non-patrician who was the first in his family to serve in the senate or be elected consul.

thievery than on good works in the path to power and political honors. It was as if a praetorship, a consulship, or any other office of this sort were noble and eminent in name only, and not only insofar as the degree of virtue of those occupying such offices. But because of my grief and anger at the state of affairs in my country, I have spoken excessively and meandered too far off the path. I now return to my subject.

V. I will record the war that the Roman people waged against Jugurtha, the king of the Numidians: first, because it was an extended and savage conflict with a dubious victory; second, because for the first time action took place to oppose the arrogance of the nobility. It was a struggle that upset the order of all things human and divine to such a degree that civil passions brought about war and the ruin of Italy. But before I actually begin to describe these events, I will revisit a few preliminaries so that the comprehension of things described here may be more readily enhanced.

In the time of the Second Punic War,[109] when the Carthaginian leader Hannibal had weakened the power of Italy most decisively since the inception of the Roman state, Masinissa, the king of Numidia, was befriended by Publius Scipio. Scipio was afterwards given the surname "Africanus" on account of his special abilities, for he had a number of impressive military deeds to his credit. Once the Carthaginians were defeated and Syphax[110] (whose holdings in Africa were large and important) was captured, the Roman people gave these lands and cities it had seized in war as a gift to Masinissa.

---

[109] The Second Punic War lasted from 218 to 202 B.C.

[110] Syphax was a western Numidian king. *See* Livy VIII.28. He changed sides and alliances often: first he was an enemy of the Carthaginians, then their friend (Livy XXIV.48 and XXVIII.17). He then went over to the Romans under Scipio, before finally switching sides again back to the Carthaginians. He was eventually captured and carried to Italy. His tomb still stands today in Batna, Algeria.

Thus our friendship with Masinissa remained useful and well-grounded. But his rule and his life came to an end at the same time. Eventually his son Micipsa became the sole ruler after his brothers Mastanabal and Gulussa wasted away through illness. Micipsa's offspring were Adherbal and Hiempsal. He also brought into the royal household—in the same way as his own sons—a boy named Jugurtha, the son of his brother Mastanabal; because Jugurtha had been the product of a relationship with a concubine, Masinissa had removed him from the royal circle to the ranks of common citizenry.

VI. When Jugurtha came of age, he was powerful in masculine traits and handsome in appearance, but most of all had a strong character. He did not give himself over to the corrupting influence of soft living and inertia but, as was customary among his people, he mastered horsemanship, practiced with the javelin, and competed with his peers in running. Even though he surpassed everyone in fame, he still remained dear to all. In addition to this he spent much time in hunting; he was the first (or among the first) to bring down lions or other big game. He accomplished much, yet spoke of himself little.

In the beginning Micipsa had been quite happy with these developments, believing that Jugurtha's virtue would bring his kingdom glory. But when he appreciated that the man was young and growing steadily in power, while he himself was getting on in years and his own children were still juveniles, he was very much troubled by the situation and turned it over constantly in his head. He was deeply uneasy in his awareness of the nature of man, which lusts after power and recklessly seeks to satisfy its inner cravings; besides this, an opportunity existed from the reality of Micipsa's and his sons' ages, something that through the hope of gain tempts even men of average ambition to ill-considered action. He also watched the growing devotion of the Numidians for Jugurtha, and grew nervous that if he were to execute such a man on some trumped-up pretext, war or rebellion might be the consequence.

VII. Beset by these difficulties, and seeing that he could not dispose of a man so embraced by the people through brute force or treachery, Micipsa resolved that because Jugurtha was ready for action and hungry for military glory, he would expose him to dangers and in this way tempt fate. Thus during the Numantine War[111] when Micipsa sent infantry and cavalry to assist the Roman people, he put Jugurtha in charge of the Numidians sent to Spain, hoping he would be killed while showing off his combat skills or through the cruelty of the enemy.

But the ultimate result was far removed from what he had anticipated. Jugurtha, who had a sharp and probing mind, soon learned both the nature of Publius Scipio (who was the Roman field commander) and the ways of the enemy. Through hard work and consistent diligence, and by showing scrupulous loyalty in placing himself in the way of danger, he quickly gained notoriety: he was much loved by our men, and was to the Numantians a constant terror. And this truly is something not easy to do: he was both vigorous in war and wise in discussion. The former may often bring rashness through audacity; and the latter, fear through excessive prudence. The Roman commander included Jugurtha in nearly all his difficult tasks and even befriended him; his affection grew on a daily basis, as the Numidian undertook no plan or enterprise without profit. To this was added his greatness of soul and resourcefulness of character, things which attached many Romans to him in close friendship.

VIII. In our army at that time there were a good number of self-made men and nobles for whom riches were more important than integrity and honesty. Seditious at home, domineering

---

[111] The siege of the city of Numantia (located just north of the modern Spanish city of Soria) took place over a thirteen month period from 134 to 133 B.C., and was the final chapter in Rome's conquest of Spain. Scipio Aemilianus was the Roman commander, and presided over the destruction of the city.

towards our allies, and more well-known than reputable, these men ignited Jugurtha's gifted mind by promising that if Micipsa were to die, he could make himself the sole ruler of Numidia. He possessed the best character, while at Rome everything was open to bribery.

But after Numantia had been crushed, Publius Scipio dismissed his auxiliaries and decided to return to Rome himself; he rewarded Jugurtha with gifts and praised him before troop formations. He then brought him to his general's tent and strongly advised the young man to cultivate the friendship of the Roman people as a whole rather than the favor of private parties, and not to get in the habit of trafficking in bribes with such persons. He believed it was dangerous to buy from a few what belonged to the many. If he would continue on his present course, he counseled Jugurtha, glory and kingly power would eventually come; but if he moved too quickly, he would come to a precipitous end with the help of his own money.

IX. Scipio then dismissed him after having said these things, and gave him a letter intended for Micipsa. The gist of the letter was this: "The martial prowess of your Jugurtha in the Numantine War was of the highest quality, which I know you will be most pleased to hear. He is most valuable to us because of his merit; and we will make every effort to ensure that the senate and the Roman people see him in the same way. Indeed, I give you thanks for our friendship: you have here a man worthy of your name and the name of your grandfather Masinissa."

So the king—when he learned from the general's letter that the rumors about Jugurtha could be confirmed—then softened his stance, persuaded by the young man's popularity and by his own strength of character. He tried to win him over by friendly overtures; he adopted him immediately and made him a co-equal beneficiary of his will along with his sons. But a few years later, when infirmity and sickness had taken their toll and he realized that his life's end was approaching, he is said to have spoken these words to Jugurtha in the presence of his family, friends, and two sons Adherbal and Hiempsal:

X. "When you were a young boy, Jugurtha, and without a father, opportunity, or resources, I brought you into my kingdom, believing that from this generosity you would cherish me no less than if I had begot you myself. And my opinion was not wrong. Without even mentioning your other great and exceptional accomplishments, lately after coming back from Numantia you have honored my kingdom with glory. Through your virtue you have made our friends the Romans even more friendly; in Spain, the name of our royal family has been given new luster. And finally, you have conquered jealousy with glory, a most difficult thing for a man to do.[112]

"Now that nature is bringing my life to a close—and with this raised right hand invoking loyalty to the kingdom—I warn and implore you to hold dear these youths who are your blood relations and, through my favor, your brothers. Do not prefer taking into your heart others outside the family, than retaining those joined to you by blood. Neither armies nor treasure-vaults are the guardians of a kingdom, but true friends, which you can neither force with arms nor buy with gold. They are acquired only by responsibility and loyalty. Who is more well-disposed than a brother to his own brother? What outsider will you find to be loyal to you, if you make an enemy of your family? Without doubt I pass on to you a secure kingdom if you are good, but a fragile one if you act badly. With domestic amity, even small nations can grow great; but discord can cripple the most impressive realms.[113]

"Because you are older and more experienced than these boys, Jugurtha, it is right that you should take care that my wishes are

───────────────────

[112] *Postremo, quod difficillumum inter mortalis est, gloria invidiam vicisti.* The gist is that Jugurtha's glory has enabled him to master the human weakness of envying others.

[113] This was a famous Sallustian maxim of the Renaissance: *Nam concordia parvae res crescunt, discordia maximae dilabuntur.*

carried out. For in every contest, he who has the greater resources is seen as the one in control, even if he is suffering injury. As for you, Adherbal and Hiempsal, support and learn from this great man here; emulate his manly virtues, and work hard so that I am not seen as having adopted better children than I gave birth to."

XI. Although Jugurtha perceived that the king's words were disingenuous (and although he himself was planning a very different course of action than what the king wanted), he responded for the time being in a conciliatory way. Micipsa died a few days later. After his people performed the funerary rites in the usual sumptuous manner of the kingdom, the princes convened a meeting so that they could dispose of the critical issues among themselves. But Hiempsal, who was the youngest, was arrogant by nature. Even before this he had condescended to Jugurtha's common origins because he was of non-royal blood on his mother's side; now he took the seat to Adherbal's right side so that Jugurtha could not sit between the two of them, a position the Numidians consider a badge of respect. But after being chided by his brother to show due respect for Jugurtha's seniority, he was reluctantly moved to another seat at the table.

In the course of discussing many issues related to the kingdom's administration, Jugurtha suggested as one of his proposals that they ought to rescind all decrees and edicts passed within the past five years. Micipsa was, he believed, of unsound mind during this time. At this point Hiempsal said he agreed: for it was within the past three years, he declared, that Jugurtha had been adopted and come into his regal inheritance. This cutting remark penetrated deeper into Jugurtha's breast than anyone could have believed. From this moment forward he was consumed with resentment and anxiety; he initiated plans and preparations through which Hiempsal might be neutralized by stratagem. But his designs advanced too slowly; his indomitable spirit remained unappeased; and he resolved to carry out his intentions in any manner he could.

XII. Due to the dissension at the first meeting that I have described above, the three princes resolved to divide the resources of the kingdom and to set up separate regions of control. Thus a time for completing each of these objectives was agreed on; dividing up the money was the earlier of the two. The princes arrived separately to an agreed location near the treasury. Now by chance Hiempsal was using a house in the town of Thirmida that was owned by one of Jugurtha's aides,[114] a man who had always been very dear and important to him. This convenient agent—provided by chance—Jugurtha filled with promises; he directed the aide to go to the house, look it over, and have duplicate door keys made.[115] The original keys were provided to Hiempsal, who confirmed he would arrive at the appointed place with a large detachment of soldiers. The Numidian aide carried out his orders and let Jugurtha's soldiers into the house at night, just as he had been instructed.

The soldiers quickly moved through the house, splitting into groups to look for the king; they killed some occupants who were sleeping, and others who put up a fight; they searched hiding-places, forced their way into locked rooms, and filled the entire house with noise and chaos. Hiempsal, terrified and unfamiliar with the layout of the house, was eventually found hiding in the living quarters of a servant-girl. The Numidians, as they had been directed, brought his head back to Jugurtha.

XIII. But then the news of this brutal murder was quickly disseminated all over Africa. Fear gripped Adherbal and all who

---

[114] The word used here is *lictor*. In Roman administrative culture this was an attendant or aide provided to a judge or other important official. Sallust's use of the words *carus* (dear) and *acceptus* (pleasing) as modifiers provides a hint that the relationship between Jugurtha and this attendant may have been an intimate one.

[115] The keys are described *adulterinas* (forged or counterfeit). I have chosen to translate this word as "duplicate"; it makes better sense in context when contrasted with the "original" or "true" (*verae*) keys.

had served under Micipsa. Numidians fell into two factions; most stood with Adherbal, but those better at warfare went with his opponent. Jugurtha outfitted the greatest number of troops he could; he brought some urban centers under his control by force and others through goodwill, and then prepared to take over all of Numidia. Although Adherbal had sent ministers to Rome to inform them of the murder of his brother and his own present situation, he nevertheless prepared to solve the problem through arms, relying on the greater number of his forces. But when battle finally came, he was defeated and fled to our African province,[116] ultimately settling in Rome.

Once Jugurtha had brought his plans to completion and was in control of all Numidia, he began to reflect on his crime in his leisure moments; he feared the response of the Roman people, and believed the only way to avoid their wrath was to make use of the nobility's greed and his own financial resources. Therefore he sent a few ministers to Rome a few days later with an ample supply of gold and silver; he directed them first to satisfy his old friends with gifts, and then reach out to new people. The goal was to do whatever could be done with lavish giving in the shortest time possible.

But when Jugurtha's ministers arrived at Rome and distributed impressive gifts (as the king had instructed) to his friends and others who wielded power in the senate at that time, such a major change occurred that the acute antagonism of the nobles was transformed into goodwill and popularity. Some were influenced by wishful thinking, others by payoffs; they pressured individual senators not to take too hard a line against Jugurtha. When the ministers were sufficiently confident, a day was set for a senatorial hearing for both sides. From what we know, Adherbal then spoke the following words:

---

[116] I.e., Roman Africa, which consisted of the coastal territory once controlled by Carthage.

XIV. "Conscript fathers, my father Micipsa warned me as he was about to die that I should think of myself as a trustee of the kingdom of Numidia; the real source of power and law came from you. At the same time, he said I should seek to be as valuable as possible to the Roman people in both civil and military matters: I should treat you as kinsmen and special neighbors. If I did this, I would have in your friendship an army, national wealth, and protections for my kingdom. As I was carrying out these lessons of my father, Jugurtha, the biggest criminal walking the earth today, expelled me—the grandson of Masinissa and a longstanding friend and ally of the Roman people—from my kingdom in contempt of your power and took all my possessions.

"Because I, conscript fathers, have come into such misery, I prefer to seek your help rather more for my own benefit than for that of my ancestors; I prefer to be obligated to the Roman people for benefits that I did not need. Alternately, if such benefits should be requested from you, I hope I might make use of what is owed. But because honesty alone offers too little protection, and because I played no role in determining what kind of man Jugurtha would be, I have appealed directly to you, conscript fathers. I am forced—and this is what is most distressing to me—to be a burden to you rather than an asset. Other kings have been granted your friendship either when they were defeated in war or when they sought an alliance to deal with dangerous conditions. Our family began its friendship with the Roman people during the Carthaginian war; this was a time when it must have been aiming at future faith more than present fortune.[117]

---

[117] *Quo tempore magis fides eius quam fortuna petunda erat.* Rome was hard-pressed during the war with Carthage and came close to losing it. So Adherbal's meaning is that "My family was in your corner when you had your back against the wall. We believed in your future more than any present benefit at the time." He masterfully plays on the senate's sense of obligation and shame.

"A little while ago I was from a royal family, powerful in name and resources; now I am beset by troubles, lacking in resources, and petitioning others for aid. If I had no other reason for appealing to you other than my desperate situation, it would still suit the greatness of the Roman people to prevent injustice and not to tolerate anyone to gain power through criminal means. I have been expelled from those lands that the Roman people gifted to my ancestors, the same lands where my father and grandfather helped you force out Syphax and the Carthaginians.[118] Your legacy has been taken away from me, conscript fathers; in my injury it is you who have been disrespected. How terrible is this situation! My father Micipsa, is there any way to undo your kindness to the person whom you made equal to your own children, and gave a share in your kingdom? This man who more than anything should prove to be the one who destroys your entire royal line?

"So will our family never find peace? Will we always be surrounded with blood, weapons, and exile? When the Carthaginians were undefeated, we of course suffered all kinds of brutality. The enemy were right next to us, and you, our friends, were a long way off. All our hope was placed in our own military capability. After that scourge was thrown out of Africa, we lived in peace happily since we had no external enemy (unless by chance you ordered us to take one on).[119] But then see what happened! Out of nowhere Jugurtha, with intolerable recklessness and driven by criminal urges and arrogance, slaughtered my brother—his own co-ruler—and made my brother's lands the first prize of his wickedness. Later, when he was unable to lure me into

---

[118] The Numidian king Syphax was allied with Carthage against Rome during the Second Punic War. In the Battle of Bagbrades (203 B.C.) the Romans under Scipio Africanus defeated a combined Carthaginian-Numidian army. Syphax played a role in this battle on the losing side.
[119] I.e., to fulfill treaty obligations with Rome and assist in her wars.

the same trap, I became—as you see me now—exiled from my ancestral lands; I wanted no part of drawn-out violence or armed conflict in your sphere of influence. This has caused my destitution and subjection to such ill-fortune that I am safer anywhere than in my own kingdom.

"Conscript fathers, I used to think—as my father also stated—that whoever cultivated your friendship sincerely took on a great responsibility but would above all else be assured of security. What was honorable about our family was that it helped you in all your wars. The fact that we are safe to enjoy leisure, conscript fathers, is due to your power. Our father left us two natural brothers; the third, Jugurtha, he hoped would be joined to us if he showered him with kindness. One of these brothers has been murdered, and I myself have barely avoided the ruthless hand of another. What should I do? To whom will I appeal in my unfortunate situation? Every protection of my family has been extinguished. My father, as was inevitable, has passed away. My brother's life was snatched away by the criminal act of a family member, an act that is deeply abhorrent. Relatives, friends, and family members have been purged by force.

"As for those captured by Jugurtha, some have been crucified, others thrown to wild animals; the few allowed to live have been imprisoned in darkness to live out a "life" worse than death amid sorrow and pain. But if everything that I have lost—or that has become alienated from me—still remained intact, I would nevertheless still petition you for help if some unexpected disaster had happened to me, conscript fathers: because of the magnitude of your empire, all legal questions of right and wrong ought to be your concern. I am truly an exile from my country and my home; I am alone and in need of all consideration that my rank permits. Who can I go to, and to whom else can I appeal? Can I go to other nations or kings? Are not these all hostile to our family because of our relationship with Rome? Where am I able to go and not see many reminders of my ancestors' hostile actions? Is it possible for anyone to have compassion for us if he was once our enemy?

"Masinissa advised us, conscript fathers, that we should not cultivate anyone except the Roman people, and should not enter into alliances or treaties with anyone else. He believed there would be a great deal of security for us within the folds of your friendship; and if your empire's fortunes were to change, we would both perish as one.

"You are great and powerful through your own virtue and the will of the gods. All things work in your favor and bend to your will. You may more easily have an opportunity to care about the injustices suffered by your allies. I am concerned, however, that private affection for Jugurtha—whose true nature is insufficiently known—may blind some of you to the truth. I am hearing that he is using a great deal of resources, visiting with you individually, and badgering you to make no decision in his absence without learning his version of events. He says I am making up stories, faking my exile, and could have stayed in my kingdom. But more than anything I would like to see that person—by whose evil actions I have been thrown into this miserable situation—try to allege this. And before it is too late, I would like to see some degree of consideration for human troubles come either from you or from the immortal gods, so that this person, who is now famous and emboldened by his crimes, will be tormented by all kinds of retributions and will pay a severe price for the betrayal of my father, the murder of my brother, and for my current destitution.

"My brother, most dear to my heart, although life has been snatched away from you as a young man in the most unjustified way possible, I believe your fate should be a source of positive hope rather than grief. When you lost your life you did not lose your kingdom; you avoided a humiliating flight, exile, deprivation, and all those hardships that now oppress me. I am in a state of grief at having been thrown out of my father's kingdom; my situation is a cautionary tale on human affairs. I am uncertain about exactly what to do: whether I should pursue those who harmed you when I myself am desperate for help, or whether I—

whose life or death hinges on the assistance of outsiders—should look after my own interests in the kingdom. I wish that dying were a respectable escape for a man in my situation; I wish—if I were just to give up, having been worn out by my injuries—that I might not be seen as living as a coward. At this point it does not much please me to live; and yet I cannot quite die without dishonor.

"Conscript fathers, help me in my predicament. Through your own influence, by your children and your parents, and through the greatness of the Roman people, prevent this injustice. Refuse to allow the kingdom of Numidia—which belongs to you—to be lost through crime and the spilled blood of our family."

XV. Once the king had finished speaking, Jugurtha's ambassadors (trusting more to bribery than to the merits of their case) responded with a few words. They claimed that Hiempsal had been assassinated by the Numidians for his tyrannical behavior; that Adherbal had provoked the war voluntarily and, once defeated, was now complaining he was unable to cause more damage. They said that Jugurtha wanted the senate to remember him as he had been thought of during the siege of Numantia, and that they should not value the words of an enemy more highly than his own record.

Finally both sides left the Curia.[120] The senate deliberated on the matter immediately. Partisans of the ambassadors, as well as a sizeable part of the senate influenced by their favors, mocked the words of Adherbal and fawned over the virtues of Jugurtha with excessive praise. With their popularity, arguments, and every other method, they bent over backwards to justify the crimes and wickedness of a foreigner as if they were advancing their own pet programs. Against this picture there were a few for whom justice and fair dealing were more important than payoffs; they believed

---

[120] The house of the Roman senate.

in aiding Adherbal and punishing severely the killing of Hiempsal. The most notable of these was Aemilius Scaurus,[121] a man of patrician background, energetic and seditious; hungry for power, honors, and wealth, he was also expert in hiding his character flaws. When he saw the king's notorious, lavish, and undisguised distributions of cash, he reined in his impulses from their usual wantonness out of fear that association with such brazen freewheeling might generate a public outcry (as is often the case).

XVI. Nevertheless, that faction in the senate which had deployed bribery and favors emerged victorious. It was ruled that ten legates should divide between Adherbal and Jugurtha the kingdom Micipsa had once presided over. Directing these legates was Lucius Opimius,[122] a formidable man and highly influential senator; during his consulship he had overseen with severity the nobles' victory over the lower classes once the killings of Caius Gracchus and Marcus Fulvius Flaccus had been carried out. Although he was one of Jugurtha's enemies at Rome, the Numidian king cultivated him with great care; he plied Opimius with expensive gifts and promises until he began to place the interests of Jugurtha ahead of his own reputation, integrity, and eventually everything else that mattered.

Jugurtha employed the same method of engagement with the other legates; only to a few of them was personal integrity more important than money. When it came to the actual division of Numidia, Jugurtha was given the section bordering Mauretania, the part that was more populous and had the better agricultural land. Adherbal received the remainder of the country; it boasted

---

[121] An apparently reputable man of patrician background. *See* Valerius Maximus III.7—8.

[122] Lucius Opimius was consul in 121 B.C. He harshly repressed the supporters of Caius Gracchus, eventually having about 3,000 of them executed.

more harbors and large buildings but was more attractive in appearance than in productive use.

XVII. The narrative here would seem to require a short explanation of conditions in Africa and its people, with whom we in Rome have had experience of both conflict and friendship. I am not easily able to give a reliable account in full of certain regions and peoples that are inaccessible, due to the heat, the harshness of the terrain, and their isolated locations. I will summarize what is reliably known in as few words as possible.

In dividing up the earth many experts assign Africa to a third geographical category; a few limit their division only to Europe and Asia, placing Africa within Europe. Africa's border on the west is the strait between the Mediterranean Sea and the Ocean; on the east it is bounded by a descending breadth of land that the natives of the region call "Catabathmos."[123] The sea is difficult to navigate and lacks good ports; the lands yield good crops and are favorable for raising animals, but are poor in forests. The sky and the earth are greatly deficient in water. The natives are healthy in body, run swiftly, and are submissive to physical labor. Most of them live to advanced ages save for those who fall victim to armed conflict or wild animals; infectious diseases rarely overcome them. There exists in Africa a large variety of dangerous animals.

I will provide a few sparse words regarding what peoples originally occupied Africa, who arrived after them, and in what way the nationalities mixed with each other. My views in this regard diverge somewhat from accepted tradition; but they correspond with the Punic-language sources (said to have been authored by king Hiempsal[124]) that have been translated for me,

---

[123] For *mare nostrum* I use "Mediterranean Sea." Catabathmos is a Greek term describing a region in Libya near Egypt. Sallust apparently considers Egypt more culturally tied to the Near East in Asia than to "Africa."

[124] This is not the Hiempsal (brother of Adherbal) featured in the present

and these are in agreement with what natives of that land believe. My account's factual accuracy will, however, depend on the reliability of these authorities.

XVIII. Africa was originally populated by Gaetulians and Libyans, who were uncultivated and rough peoples; these subsisted on the flesh of wild beasts and on foraging in the manner of farm animals. They had neither social systems nor legal codes and were not ruled by any central authority: roving and nomadic in their ways, they resided wherever the end of daylight forced them to stop.

But after Hercules[125] died in Spain—as the Africans believe—his army soon melted away; it was composed of men of many ethnicities and had various rival claimants for power now that their leader was gone. The Medes, Persians, and Armenians of his army crossed into Africa by ships and colonized the areas close to our sea,[126] with the Persians adjacent to the Ocean.[127] They used the inverted hulls of their ships for shelter since there were no other raw materials available in that terrain. Neither could the Persians buy or barter anything from the Spaniards; the vastness of the sea-distances and their inability to speak the local language prevented commerce. Little by little, the Persians mingled with the Gaetulians through marriage; and because they often moved around in search of better lands, they called themselves "Nomads."[128] We may note that the houses of Numidians (which

work, but a different king of the same name. Sallust refers here to Hiempsal II, the son of Gauda and the father of Juba I. His dates of birth and death are not precisely known, but he was deposed as king of Numidia in 81 B.C.

[125] Many classical writers accepted Hercules as an actual historical figure. We cannot be sure they were wrong.

[126] I.e., the Mediterranean.

[127] The Atlantic.

[128] There are two variations of this word: *Nomades* and *Nomas*. It appears not only in Sallust but also in Virgil (*Aen.* IV.320 and VIII.724). According to the

they call *mapalia*) in rural areas even now retain oblong roofs with curved sides, just like the hulls of boats.

The Medes, however, settled closer to the Libyans, who themselves were not very far from the African Sea.[129] The Gaetulians lived farther south near the desert wastes. In a short time these newcomers had established towns; and separated from Spain only by the straits, they soon began to develop commercial relations with the inhabitants there. The Libyans little by little corrupted their original name until eventually "Medes" became "Moors" in their barbarian language.[130]

The original Persian colony grew larger in a short time. The surplus population caused some of them—under the name Numidians—to migrate from their original home into the region of land near Carthage that is called Numidia. Then the two of them working together brought other neighbors under their control by force or through fear; they gained a reputation for military glory, especially those who were living near our own sea, since the Libyans are less bellicose than the Gaetulians. Ultimately a large part of the north African coast came under Numidian control; all the subject peoples were merged into the ethnicity and name of the conquering power.

XIX. Later the Phoenicians—partly for the sake of reducing their domestic population, and partly to cater to the imperialistic impulses of their lower classes and others eager for bold new enterprises—founded the cities of Hippo, Hadrumentum,

---

Oxford Latin Dictionary (2nd ed.), the word Numidia is traceable to this term.

[129] The waters of the western Mediterranean near the African shoreline.

[130] Sallust's ethnography here is a mixture of legend and hearsay. But if the myth of Hercules was based on an actual person—which is not impossible—there may be some scattered kernels of truth in his explanation.

Lepcis,[131] and other cities along the coast.[132] These cities in a short time became quite important: although originally intended as garrison towns, they had their own special elegance. On the subject of Carthage itself I think it would be better to remain silent than say too little, since time warns me to return to my subject.

As one follows the coastline[133] we find that in the region of Catabathmos, the tract separating Egypt from Africa, the first city is Cyrene, a colony of Thera. Then one notes the two Syrtes, between which is Lepcis.[134] Finally we reach the "Altars of Philaeni," the place the Carthaginians considered the boundary between their domain and Egypt; after this came the Punic cities. Other places as far as Mauretania[135] are held by the Numidians; and closest to Spain are the Moors. Below the Numidians we find the Gaetulians, some of whom live in huts, while others follow a nomadic, uncivilized existence. Beyond them are the Ethiopians, and finally those regions scorched by the sun's rays.

At the time of the war against Jugurtha the Roman people (through local magistrates) governed the majority of the Punic cities and the lands that had until recently been ruled by the Carthaginians. Under the control of Jugurtha were the greater part of the Gaetulians and Numidia as far as the river Muluccha. King Bocchus ruled over all the Moors: he knew nothing of the Roman people besides their name, and we were ignorant of him in war or in peace before that time.

I have spoken enough of Africa and its inhabitants to suit my purposes.

---

[131] Two cities had this name (which had spelling variations): Leptis Magna (modern Lebida) and Leptis Parva (modern Lempta). See the map section, above. The names Leptis Major and Leptis Minor were also used.

[132] The Lepcis referred to here is Leptis Parva, and not Leptis Magna. Hadrumentum was located where the modern Tunisian city of Sousse is now.

[133] Moving towards the west.

[134] Leptis Magna was between Greater Syrtis and Lesser Syrtis.

[135] Both Mauretania and Mauritania are accepted spellings.

XX. Once the kingdom of Numidia had been divided and the ambassadors left Africa, and Jugurtha realized he had gained the rewards of his crime in spite of his inner fears, he was sure that what he had heard from his friends at Numantia was true: that all of Rome was open to influence through bribery. Likewise influenced by the promises of those whom he had recently enriched with gifts, he turned his attention to Adherbal's kingdom. Jugurtha was energetic and aggressive while the man he targeted was peaceful, reticent, and of a calm disposition; he was a ready-made victim, someone more inclined to fear than to be feared.

Thus without warning Jugurtha crossed into Adherbal's territory with a large force, killing many, capturing livestock and other spoils, and setting fire to structures. He made aggressive moves into many areas with his cavalry, then retreated back to his own kingdom, thinking that Adherbal would be moved by indignation to retaliate once he realized the extent of the damage done to him. This would serve as the pretext for his intended war. But because Adherbal did not believe he was equal to his opponent in military strength, and more trusted his alliance with the Roman people than he did his own Numidians, he sent delegates to Jugurtha to protest these territorial violations. Although the delegates brought back contemptuous responses, he decided it was better to tolerate everything than to declare war, since things had ended badly the previous time he had tried this option.

But Jugurtha's greed was not satiated by this; in his own mind he had already annexed Adherbal's domain. He therefore initiated hostilities, not with a raiding party as before but with a large army he had raised, and openly sought to bring all Numidia under his control. Wherever he went he ravaged cities and agricultural lands and carried off plunder; he emboldened the spirits of his own men, and struck fear in the hearts of his enemy.

XXI. When Adherbal realized what was happening and that he would either have to surrender his kingdom or keep it by fighting, he had no choice but to raise an army and move to interdict Jugurtha. Eventually both armies took up positions near the town of Cirta not far from the sea, but they did not engage each other because daylight had almost ended. When most of the night had gone (but not yet at daybreak), Jugurtha's soldiers on a given order attacked the enemy's camp. Some were half-asleep while others had just picked up their weapons: they were promptly put to flight and scattered. Adherbal fled to Cirta with a few cavalry; and had it not been for a group of civilians who prevented the Numidian pursuers from coming up to the city walls, the war between the two rival kings would have begun and ended on the same day. Jugurtha then surrounded the town and began work on attacking it with moveable siege-works, towers, and machines of all types; by making the greatest haste he hoped to preempt the arrival of the ambassadors whom, he had heard, Adherbal had dispatched to Rome before the battle.

After the Roman senate had gotten word that the two leaders were at war, three young men were sent to Africa as envoys. They were to visit with both kings and inform them that the senate and Roman people wished and decreed that the two of them should cease fighting: it was better that their dispute be resolved through binding arbitration rather than through war. This course of conduct (as they would inform the feuding Numidians) was worthy of both themselves and the Roman people.

XXII. The ambassadors came to Africa quickly, all the more so because when they were preparing to leave Rome, they heard that a battle had taken place and that Cirta was under siege. But the rumors downplayed the gravity of the situation. When Jugurtha had heard the envoys, he responded with a speech telling them how nothing was dearer or more important to him than the authority of the Roman senate. From adolescence, he said, he had worked hard to be respected by the best men; he had found favor with Publius Scipio—the greatest of men—through his quality of character and not through vice; and it was because of these same traits that he had been adopted by Micipsa, not because the king had had too few children.

129

Furthermore, he added, the more things he did that were good and noticeable, the less his spirit could tolerate injustices committed against him. Adherbal had maliciously schemed to murder him; he had discovered the plot and then revealed the crime. The Roman people would be acting neither correctly nor justly if they were to prohibit him from invoking the "law of nations."[136] He finally promised he would dispatch envoys to Rome in a short time to explain the details of what had happened. Each of them then departed. No attempt was made to speak to Adherbal's force.

XXIII. Believing he could not take Cirta by conventional assault due to its natural location, Jugurtha surrounded its walls with a rampart and a trench once he believed that the Roman envoys had left Africa. He constructed towers and fortified them with troops; day and night he tried to take the town either by force or by guile. To the defenders he alternately offered financial rewards or intimidation; he kept the combative spirit of his own men high with martial speeches and single-mindedly prepared every detail of the campaign.

When Adherbal realized that his entire situation was approaching a critical point, that his enemy could not be appeased, that there was no hope of relief, and that he could not carry on the war due to the lack of vital supplies, he selected two of the most capable men who had fled with him to Cirta. These he motivated by many promises and by pity at his desperate situation, directing them to slip through the enemy's siege-works at night, head towards the nearest coast, and from there proceed to Rome.

XXIV. His Numidians carried out these orders within a few days. Adherbal's letter was read in the senate; it conveyed the following message.

---

[136] This is the *ius gentium*, a kind of universal "natural law" based on principles of accepted morality. See Cicero, *De officiis* III.17.

"It is not my fault that I come before you to speak so often, conscript fathers. Jugurtha's violence compels me; he is consumed with such a lust for my destruction that he cares neither for you nor the immortal Gods. He desires my blood above all else. Although a friend and ally of the Roman people, I have been held in a military siege for four months now. Neither the services done by my father Micipsa nor your previous decisions have been of any use to me; and I do not know whether I am hounded more by hunger or by arms.

"My present circumstance advises me against writing more about Jugurtha. I have also learned in my life that little confidence is placed in someone who has fallen on hard times. I have come to believe that he wants more than what I am seeking; he does not want both your friendship and my kingdom. Which of these two he considers more important is hidden to no one. He first killed my brother Hiempsal, then expelled me from my own kingdom. Of course these events were our own domestic concerns, not yours; but now he holds your protectorate kingdom by military occupation. I, whom you set up as leader of Numidia, am now under siege. My desperate situation shows how much he has cared about the statements of your envoys. What is left that can change the situation, besides your power?

"I would certainly prefer that these words I now write—and those that I spoke to you previously in the senate—were untrue, rather than that they be confirmed by my desperation. But since I now live in order to be a showcase for Jugurtha's crimes, I no longer pray to escape death or hardship, but only that I avoid the tyranny of an enemy or bodily torture. Do what you wish regarding the kingdom of Numidia—which belongs to you—but rescue me from impious hands. I ask this by the greatness of your empire and by my trust in your friendship, if anything lingers in your memory of my grandfather Masinissa."

XXV. When this letter was read there were those who thought an army should be sent to Africa to help Adherbal as soon as practicable; in the interim, they thought, notice should be taken of Jugurtha's having ignored the Roman envoys. But those same supporters of the king[137] exerted every effort to prevent such a resolution from being passed. Thus the common good, as often happens in such matters, was defeated by private interests. Nevertheless important senior officials serving in prominent positions were dispatched to Africa: one of these was Marcus Scaurus (whom we have already noted), a man who had held consular rank and who was now the senate leader.[138]

Responding to public anger and the pleadings of the Numidians, these men boarded ships within three days. They soon after put ashore at Utica and sent a letter to Jugurtha saying that they had been sent to him by the senate, and that he should come to the province as quickly as possible.[139] When he heard that important men whose authority in Rome was said to be considerable had arrived to disrupt his plans, he was initially thrown off his game; he then alternated between fear and opportunistic hunger. He was afraid of the senate's ire if he did not comply with the envoys; at the same time his mind, consumed by greed, was driving him to finish his crime. Corrupt counsel triumphed in his insatiable heart.

He therefore surrounded Cirta with his army and made an all-out effort to capture it, hoping that by stretching the enemy's forces to their breaking point he would be able to produce a victory either by force or trickery. When this plan did not work out and he was unable to get his hands on Adherbal before meeting the Roman envoys, he came into our province with a few

---

[137] I.e., Jugurtha's supporters in the senate already noted above.

[138] The title was *princeps senatus*. It was a high honor, often held for life. *See* Livy XXXIV.44.

[139] Utica, originally founded by the Phoenicians, became an important Roman colony after Carthage was defeated. Its ruins still exist in modern Tunisia near Bizerte where the Medjerda River empties into the Mediterranean.

cavalry so that Scaurus—a man whom he very much feared—would not become irritated by waiting too long. Although serious warnings were conveyed in the senate's name, the Roman envoys departed without success since Jugurtha would not lift the siege.

XXVI. When these events became known at Cirta, the Italic inhabitants—on whose bravery the defense of the town had depended—persuaded Adherbal to deliver the town and himself into Jugurtha's hands; an agreement would be made for his personal safety and the remaining terms would be the concern of the senate. The Italic colonists were confident that in the event of surrender they themselves would be safe because of Rome's authority. Although Adherbal reckoned that anything would be better than trusting to Jugurtha's good faith, he still surrendered as the colonists advised, knowing that they had the ability to force him to do so if he refused. Jugurtha immediately tortured Adherbal to death; he then undertook the wholesale slaughter of all adult Numidians and merchants who had taken up arms.

XXVII. When word of these events reached Rome and the senate began to debate them, the same agents of the king minimized the atrocities that had been committed by interrupting others and using argumentation to waste time. Had not Caius Memmius (the elected tribune of the plebs), a keenly intelligent man opposed to the power of the nobility, explained to the Roman people that the gridlock was an attempt to whitewash Jugurtha's crimes by a few of his senatorial collaborators, certainly all ill-feeling would have melted away as a result of the protracted debates. Such was the power of the king's money and influence.

But since the senate—due to its guilty conscience—was afraid of the people, Numidia and Italy were assigned to the consuls who should next come into office in accordance with the Sempronian law.[140] The consuls chosen were Publius Scipio Nasica and Lucius Calpurnius Bestia; Calpurnius received Numidia, and Scipio got Italy. Finally an army was raised that would be transported to Africa; military payrolls and the other logistical requirements needed for war were also ordered.

XXVIII. But this news came to Jugurtha against his expectations, for it was stuck in his mind that at Rome everything would go his way. He sent his son with two friends as representatives to the senate with the same game-plan he gave those who were sent after the killing of Hiempsal: he told them to approach everyone with offers of money. As they came closer to Rome, Bestia asked the senate whether it would be appropriate to receive Jugurtha's envoys inside the city. The senate eventually ruled that unless the representatives had come to hand over the king and his kingdom, they should leave Italy within the next ten days. The consul ordered that the senate's ruling should be delivered to the Numidians; they thus returned home without accomplishing their goal.

Meanwhile Calpurnius, after raising his army, entrusted its operation to nobles of his own political party with whose assistance he hoped that any misconduct could be swept under the rug. One of these was Scaurus; we have described his nature and habits in preceding pages.[141] Our consul had many good qualities of mind and body, but ultimately all of them were dominated by greed. He had a strong capacity for work, a sharp mind, good foresight, combat experience, and was very resolute in the face of dangers and confrontations. The legions were transported across Italy to Rhegium, then to Sicily, and finally to Africa. After securing his logistics Calpurnius moved forcefully into Numidia;

---

[140] An agrarian reform law dating from the time of Caius Gracchus. Among other things, it held that provinces should be watched over by consuls before the consular elections.
[141] See XV.

he then began combat operations against many enemy units and towns.

XXIX. But when Jugurtha through his representatives offered him bribes and began to make clear the hardships of the war he was getting involved in, Calpurnius's mind—corrupted by greed—was easily deflected from its task. Scaurus was brought along as an accomplice and a supporter of all his plans. In the beginning many in his political faction had been corrupted; he had fought the king vigorously; but eventually he was drawn away from honesty and integrity to crookedness by the sheer volume of money offered. At first Jugurtha was only able to delay the onset of war, thinking he might be able to produce some positive result in Rome with bribery or favoritism. But when he heard that Scaurus was a participant in the negotiations, he was seized with a great hope for a peaceful settlement, and so decided to go in person to discuss all relevant issues with the envoys.

In the meantime, the quaestor Sextius was sent by the consul to Vaga (a town belonging to Jugurtha) as evidence of good faith. The declared purpose of the mission was to receive stocks of grain that Calpurnius had demanded from the envoys as part of a truce until a formal surrender could be negotiated. As he had promised, the king came to the camp; he delivered a few remarks in the presence of the council about the bad acts committed and offered his surrender. The remaining issues he discussed privately with Bestia and Scaurus. On the next day he was accepted in surrender after the outstanding issues had been more or less hammered out.[142] As had been ordered by the council, thirty elephants, many cattle and horses, and a small quantity of silver were given to the quaestor. Calpurnius departed for Rome to participate in the civil elections. Peace prevailed in Numidia and for our army.

---

[142] Sallust makes it clear that the decision-making was not a model of thoroughness: *Dein postero die, quasi per saturam sententiis exquisitis, in deditionem accipitur.*

XXX. After the news of events in Africa—and how these events took place—was disseminated at Rome, the consul's action was the talk of every gathering. The lower classes were outraged, but the senators were apprehensive: they could not agree whether to endorse the scandal or to overturn the consul's ruling. Most influential was the power of Scaurus that blocked the pursuit of justice and truth: he functioned as the enabler and accomplice of Bestia. The senate waffled and delayed; but Caius Memmius, whose independent spirit and dislike of the nobility's power we discussed earlier, urged the people through public speeches to avenge the injustices done. He warned them not to abandon their republic or their liberty, and pointed out the many arrogant and malicious deeds of the nobility: in every way he set his mind to stirring up the passions of the plebs.

Since the eloquence of Memmius at Rome in those days was celebrated and powerful, I have thought it useful to reproduce one of his many speeches. I will transcribe the most potent of these; namely, the public address given after the return of Bestia. His words were as follows.

XXXI. "If devotion to one's country were not more important than anything else, Quirites,[143] many things would hold me back from speaking to you: the resources of the ruling party, your acquiescence in things, the lawless situation, and most importantly the fact that more danger than respect comes from displaying integrity. Some things I am truly ashamed to speak of: how for the past fifteen years you have been the laughingstock of a few men's arrogance; how terribly your defenders perished with no consequences for the guilty; how your spirits have been so corrupted by weakness and inaction that even now you do not stir

---

[143] This rhetorical word was used in formal speeches or writing to mean the "Roman people" in a collective sense. See, e.g., Horace, *Carmina* IV.14; Pliny, *Hist. Nat.* XXXIII.134.

yourselves against a guilty enemy, but rather fear those who themselves ought to be afraid.

"But although these are the realities, my spirit nevertheless compels me to resist the power of this political faction. No matter what, I will make use of the freedom[144] that was passed down to me from my parents. It lies in your hands, Quirites, whether I do so in vain or in fulfillment of a useful purpose. I do not ask you to take up arms against injustices, as your ancestors often did; neither violence nor secession is needed. They[145] should go over the cliff as a result of their own behaviors. After the assassination of Tiberius Gracchus, whom they accused of trying to become a king, official investigations were conducted against people of the Roman lower classes.[146] After Caius Gracchus[147] and Marcus Fulvius[148] were killed, many men of your social class met their own deaths in prison. In each situation the end of the slaughter came not by law but by the will of the ruling party.

"But certainly to restore the rights of the plebs will be equivalent to a striving for sovereignty.[149] Whatever cannot be avenged without the blood of citizens has been rightly done.[150] In previous years you silently disapproved of the robbing of the treasury, of the fact that kings and free people paid tribute to a few

---

[144] As in "freedom of speech."

[145] I.e., the leaders of the ruling faction.

[146] Gracchus, a tribune of the people, was murdered in 133 B.C. after trying to push agrarian reforms that would have threatened the power and wealth of the nobility. After his death many of his followers were hunted down and killed or exiled.

[147] Caius Sempronius Gracchus (154—121 B.C.) was, like his brother Tiberius, also killed in civil strife.

[148] Marcus Fulvius Flaccus was an ally of the Gracchi and was killed during a political protest in Rome in 121 B.C.

[149] A striving for absolute power. *Paratio regni* has been translated here as "striving for sovereignty."

[150] Meaning that justice requires the blood of citizens (i.e., violence).

aristocrats, and that those same people had the greatest fame and most extensive wealth. Yet it is not enough for them to have done these crimes with impunity; ultimately the laws, your dignity, and all things human and divine have been given to your enemies. Those who have done these things are neither ashamed nor sorry. They strut around in front of your faces, bragging, showing off their priesthoods, consulships, and their triumphs as if these things were legitimate achievements and not plunder.

"Slaves bought for some price do not tolerate the unjust control of their owners. Will you, Quirites—who were born to lead—accept slavery willingly? Who are these people who have grabbed the republic? They are the most criminal of men: men with bloodstained hands, men of consuming greed, men guilty and at the same time totally arrogant, men for whom honesty, distinction, piety, and ultimately everything honest and dishonest are avenues for personal profit. For their protection some of them have murdered tribunes of the plebs; others have set up kangaroo courts;[151] and many of them have killed *you yourselves*. Whoever acts the most wickedly is the one who is the most safe. Fear has been transplanted from their criminality to your own timidity;[152] they are forced to act as one unit since they desire, hate, and fear the same things. Among good men these things indicate friendship; among bad men they indicate a partisan faction.

"For if you cared as much about freedom as they get excited by power, then without doubt the republic would not be lying in ruins as it is now, and your sympathies would belong to the best men, rather than to the most reckless. To get their legal rights and establish popular sovereignty, your ancestors twice armed

---

[151] The phrase here is *quaestiones iniustas*. "Unjust tribunals" is adequate, but "kangaroo courts" carries a better oratorical ring.

[152] Meaning, "instead of the rulers feeling fear because of their crimes, you yourselves feel fear because of your timidity."

themselves and occupied the Aventine Hill through secession.[153] Won't you give every ounce of effort to keep this liberty that you inherited from them? And won't you fight that much harder, since it is more dishonorable to lose what has been gained than never to have gotten it at all?

"Someone may say, 'Then what do you suggest?' That those who handed over their country to the enemy must be punished. Not by arms or violence—which is more unworthy for you to do than for them to receive—but by an official inquiry and Jugurtha's own testimony. If he is a prisoner of war, he will certainly respond to your orders. But if he refuses, you can then ask yourselves: what kind of peace or surrender is it that gives Jugurtha immunity for his crimes? That gives a few powerful men a huge amount of riches? That allows our republic to suffer damage and dishonor? Unless perhaps you haven't yet had enough of their domination, and you're more satisfied with the time when kingdoms, provinces, legal systems, courts, war and peace, and finally all things human and divine belonged only to a few; and when you, the Roman people, undefeated by its enemies, rulers of all nations, were satisfied just to stay alive! For who among you dared to refuse slavery?

"Even though I consider it most shameful for a man to accept an injury without avenging it, I might still allow you with a clean conscience to forgive these utterly criminally-minded men—since they are fellow citizens—were it not for the fact that mercy would end in disaster. For they have such a lack of consideration for

---

[153] This refers to the *secessio plebis*, or "plebian secession" of Rome's early days where the lower classes would halt all trade and leave the city. The idea was to show the nobles that they could bring Rome to a standstill. Sallust errs here; there was only one secession (not two) to the Aventine Hill. This took place in 449 B.C. An earlier secession to the Mons Sacer occurred in 494 B.C. There were several others with the last recorded instance taking place in 287 B.C.

others that it is hardly enough to have committed crimes with impunity without also taking from you the ability to do more wrongdoing in the future. And you will be in a state of permanent anxiety knowing you must either be a slave or preserve your freedom with force.

"So what hope is there for trust and mutual understanding? They want to dominate you, and you want to be free. They want to cause harm, and you want to prevent it. They treat our allies as enemies, and our enemies as allies. Can there be peace and friendship between purposes so different? For this reason I warn and advise you not to let such a terrible crime go unpunished. It was not the embezzlement of public funds or the forcible taking of money from our allies: although these are serious matters, they mean little, since they have become so routine.

"The authority of the senate has been turned over to a devious enemy: and this surrendered authority is *your* authority. At home and on the field of battle, our republic was on sale to the highest bidder. Unless this is acknowledged—unless the guilty face justice—what will be left for us except to live as obedient servants to those who committed these acts? For to do whatever one likes without consequences: this is the definition of a king. I am not asking you, Quirites, to favor your fellow citizens who have acted wrongly over those who have acted rightly; I ask that you do not ruin the good ones by forgiving the bad. In a republic it is much better to forget a favor than an offense. When you fail to notice a good man, he only becomes less energetic; but overlook a bad one, and he becomes more evil. It is obvious that if there were no bad acts, you would not so often need assistance."[154]

XXXII. Through these and other like-minded statements said repeatedly, Memmius convinced the people that the praetor Lucius Cassius should be sent to Jugurtha; he was told to bring

---

[154] Meaning that if the rulers were not involved in corruption, the people would not need to take extraordinary actions to solve the problems created by the corruption.

him to Rome under a personal safety guarantee, so that the testimony of the king might more easily shed light on the actions of Scaurus and the others under indictment for receiving bribes.

While these events were happening at Rome, those left by Bestia in charge of the army in Numidia—in accordance with the habit of their leader—committed many infamous acts. There were those who, corrupted by money, gave the army's elephants back to Jugurtha; others sold him his deserters; and a part scavenged for spoils among peaceful civilians. Such was the power of the greed that had poisoned their minds like a spreading rot.

When the proposed measure of Caius Memmius was passed (to the dismay of the entire nobility), the praetor Cassius made contact with Jugurtha. Despite the king's suspicions and the wariness that grew from his sense of guilt, he assured Jugurtha that since he had given himself up to the Roman people, he would be better off learning about their mercy than experiencing their force. He also offered Jugurtha his own private guarantee of safe conduct; such at this time was Cassius's prestige.

XXXIII. So Jugurtha, shedding the dignity of a king, came to Rome with Cassius while carrying himself with the most pathetic—rather than the most regal—deportment. And although he had unwavering confidence in himself and was assured by all those through whose influence or culpability he had done the things I described above, he still bribed the tribune of the plebs Caius Baebius with a large sum of money. Through Baebius's shamelessness he thought he might be safeguarded against legal action and personal injury.

But when Caius Memmius brought the matter up for a hearing, the people were hostile to the king with some calling for his arrest; others thought that he should be punished in the fashion of our ancestors unless he named his associates in crime. Restraining their anger and calming their passions, Memmius favored prudence over rage; he assured them that the public trust would not be broken during his tenure. Then, when silence had settled over the meeting, Jugurtha was brought in. Memmius then spoke and reminded everyone of the king's actions at Rome and in Numidia, calling attention to his crimes against his father and brothers. He stated that although the Roman people knew through whose assistance and enabling the king had committed these acts, it still wanted to hear testimony from him personally. If he spoke the truth, he could place great hope in the good faith and clemency of the Roman people. But if he refrained from speaking, he would destroy his hopes and himself, and there would likewise be no safety for his associates.

XXXIV. When Memmius finished his address and Jugurtha was ordered to respond, the tribune of the people Caius Baebius—who as we noted above had been bought off—told the king not to speak. The crowd that had come to witness the hearings tried to rattle Baebius with passionate yelling, body language, and often by personal attacks: all those things that follow from swelling rage. Nevertheless his insolence won out. So the populace left the meeting having been played for fools; but Jugurtha, Bestia, and the others who were worried about the investigation had their spirits lifted.

XXXV. There was in Rome at this time a Numidian named Massiva, a son of Gulussa and a grandson of Masinissa, who in the conflict between the kings had aligned himself against Jugurtha; after the surrender of Cirta and the killing of Adherbal he had left his country as a refugee. Spurius Albinus, who (the year after Bestia) occupied the consulship along with Quintus Minucius Rufus, convinced Massiva to petition the senate for the Numidian throne since he was a descendant of Masinissa and Jugurtha was surrounded by fear and hatred for his crimes. The consul was excited about waging war and preferred action to inaction in all things. To him came the province of Numidia, and to Minucius went Macedonia.[155]

---

[155] In accordance with the provisions of the Sempronian law that assigned a province to each consul.

When Massiva began to take steps to carry out these plans, Jugurtha realized there was little enthusiasm for the project among his friends; some were impeded by their consciences, others by unacceptable notoriety and fear. Jugurtha thus ordered Bomilcar, the man nearest and most trusted by him, to contract the services of assassins by spreading around money (with which he had already done so much): and if he were unable to do this in secrecy, then he should kill the Numidian by any possible means.

Bomilcar followed the directions of the king without delay; and through men practiced in such arts he discovered his target's comings, goings, and finally his location at any time of day. Finally when the chance presented itself, he sprang his trap. One of the men hired to do the killing advanced a little too rashly on Massiva. He killed him but was himself caught; and at the urging of many interrogators—especially the consul Albinus—he eventually gave evidence. Bomilcar's indictment came about more as a result of equitable principles than by operation of the law of nations, since he was an associate of someone who had come to Rome under a "public trust."[156]

But although Jugurtha was clearly responsible for the assassination, he tried to avoid the reality of the matter until finally coming to grips with the fact that the hatred that had grown against him exceeded his celebrity and money. Therefore, although at the outset of the trial he had given fifty of his friends as sureties to the court,[157] he sent Bomilcar secretly to Numidia, caring more about preserving his regal power than about the sureties. He feared that if he had to endure some punishment, the rest of his people might no longer accept his leadership. A few days later he himself departed, having been ordered by the senate

---

[156] *Fide publica*, or a public guarantee of good faith.

[157] Defendants at trials in Rome could provide actual persons as "bonds" to the court while they themselves could enjoy being "out on bail." Such sureties were held in custody to assure the appearance of the defendant at trial.

to leave Italy. But after leaving Rome, he is supposed to have looked back frequently at Rome in silence and said, "If the right buyer comes along, this city is a corrupt one, and one that will soon be destroyed."

XXXVI. In the meantime once Albinus had renewed the war he moved quickly to bring supplies, payroll funds, and other necessities of military campaigns to Africa. He set out immediately to bring the war to a successful conclusion—by force, negotiated peace, or in any other way—before the elections were to be held, a time that was not far off. In opposition to this goal, Jugurtha wanted to prolong everything as much as he could; he created one excuse after another to drag things out. He would ask for surrender and then pretend to be afraid; he would withdraw quickly and then threaten an attack (so that his men's morale would not sag). He confused the consul by both the stratagems of war and the chicanery of negotiations.

There were some who were of the opinion that Albinus was not in the dark about the king's maneuverings; they did not accept that a war begun with such urgency could so easily be dragged out. To them, the ineptitude of the consul more than the craftiness of the king must be the explanation. But after some time had passed and the day of the elections approached, Albinus left for Rome after leaving his brother Aulus in camp as praetor.[158]

XXXVII. In Rome at that time the republic was seriously afflicted by the sedition of its tribunes. Both Publius Lucullus and Lucius Annius were making efforts to extend their terms of office against the wishes of their colleagues; this political squabble prevented the holding of elections for the entire year. This delay provided Aulus—who as I said above had been left in Africa in

---

[158] One of the jobs of the praetor was to command an army in the field. When Albinus left for Rome, he left Aulus in command of the military forces in Africa.

command of the troops—with the hope of either finishing the war or extracting a bribe from the king through fear of his military capability. For this reason he formed up his soldiers for an expedition in the month of January during the winter season; through an extended series of movements in bitter winter he came to the town of Suthul, where the king's treasure-hoard was located.

But because of the harshness of the season and the difficulty of the terrain, he was able neither to capture the town nor put it to siege. Around the city wall—constructed along a steep overhang—was a marshy plateau that had been transformed into a total swamp by the winter rains. Whether he desired to stage a mock assault in order to scare the king or, blinded by greed, he simply wished to get his hands on the town's repository of treasure, he brought in protective screens for the soldiers;[159] he constructed a causeway and moved quickly to arrange the other things that would be of use for an attack.

XXXVIII. But Jugurtha, cognizant of the foolishness and ineptitude of the Roman commander, cunningly stoked his fixation; again and again he sent him obsequious envoys while he himself led his army through wooded thickets and footpaths as if he were taking evasive action. Finally he enticed Aulus with the prospect of peace. He was to abandon the siege of Suthul and, as if he were retreating, follow the king to an isolated region of the countryside. In such a place crimes could be kept more secret.[160] Meanwhile, through the use of clever spies, he plotted day and night to corrupt Aulus's army: some centurions and unit commanders he bribed to be derelict in their duties, while others were to abandon their posts at a prearranged signal.

---

[159] The word used is *vinea*, a siege device (mantlet) made of wood and animal hides that shielded attacking soldiers from the missiles of defenders.
[160] Meaning that any unauthorized deal made between Jugurtha and Aulus would have less chance of being known.

When these preparations had been put in place, he surrounded Aulus's camp with a detachment of Numidians in the dead of night without warning. The Roman soldiers were dismayed by the unusual commotion; some took up arms, some concealed themselves, and some reassured those who were alarmed. Trepidation permeated the entire camp. The enemy force was powerful; the sky was darkened by night and clouds. Each course of action held danger: whether it was safer to flee or to stand and fight was not at all clear.

Then out of those who had been bribed (as I described above), a cohort of Ligurians, two *turmae*[161] of Thracians, and a few rank-and-file soldiers defected to the king. The chief centurion of the Third Legion permitted the enemy to enter in the sector he was tasked with defending; and there all the Numidians smashed through. Our men were put to flight in pathetic fashion with many throwing down their weapons and seeking safety on a hill that was nearby. The onset of nightfall and the enemy's plundering of the camp delayed he Numidians and somewhat diminished their victory.

Finally on the following day Jugurtha conducted a dialogue with Aulus. He said that although he was in a position to force either starvation or military destruction on his army, he was mindful of humanitarian concerns; and if Aulus would conclude a treaty with him, he would allow all the Romans to pass under the yoke unharmed.[162] Aulus would also have to leave Numidia

---

[161] The *turma* was a cavalry unit of the Roman army. During the republican period its size was probably not much more than thirty men. It would have been headed by a centurion with the help of an *optio* and a *vexillarius*.

[162] "Passing under the yoke" (*passum sub iugum*) was a very old Roman surrender ritual. To drive home the point of their defeat, enemy soldiers would be forced to walk under a yoke of elevated spears. The ritual may originally have had a quasi-religious purpose to expunge the "guilt" of the defeated.

within ten days. Although these terms were very much shameful and oppressive, nevertheless, because they were extended as a substitute for the possibility of death, peace was concluded on the king's conditions.

XXXIX. When these events became known in Rome, fear and anguish gripped the public mind. Some grieved for the empire's prestige; others unfamiliar with military affairs feared for their liberty. Everyone was enraged at Aulus—especially those who had distinguished themselves in war—since despite being armed he sought safety through humiliation rather than through resistance. So the consul Albinus, fearing a backlash from his brother's crimes and the peril that would result from this, put the treaty issue[163] before the senate. Meanwhile he petitioned for additional military aid and sent for reinforcements from Rome's allies and other Latin communities: in handling every detail of the crisis he showed a sense of urgency.

The senate ruled—as was proper[164]—that there could no treaty without both its and the people's approval. The consul, barred by the tribunes of the plebs from taking with him the military forces he had called up, departed for Africa within a few days. As had been agreed, the entire army had withdrawn from Numidia to spend the winter in the province of Roman Africa.[165] Although upon arriving Albinus was burning with a desire to expunge the shame caused by his brother's conduct, he decided after weighing his resources that he should do nothing. He knew his soldiers; and he was aware that besides the rout they had

---

[163] The treaty between Aulus and Jugurtha.

[164] The phrase "as was proper" could conceivably have another shade of meaning. Sallust here writes *uti par fuerat*: the word *par* can mean either "right" or "suitable" as well as a "co-equal pairing of two." The subtlety of Sallust's prose enables him to convey in one phrase the idea that the senate's ruling was both "right" and that the people and the senate were co-equal partners in political authority.

[165] I.e., in the province under Roman control.

suffered, discipline had broken down, and they had gone soft through lascivious conduct and disorderly behavior.

XL. Meanwhile at Rome the tribune of the plebs Caius Mamilius Limetanus publicly announced a proposed measure directed against (1) those who had advised Jugurtha to ignore senatorial decrees; (2) those who had taken money from him while serving as legates or military commanders; (3) those who had given elephants and deserters back to Jugurtha; and (4) those who had negotiated terms of peace and war with the enemy. Against this proposal were aligned both those who knew they belonged to one of these categories and those who feared class antagonism.[166] But because they could not fight it openly without revealing their acquiescence in these and other scandalous acts, they stonewalled it behind the scenes through proxies, especially through men of the Latin communities and the Italic allies. Yet with an extraordinary show of drive and purpose, the plebs passed the measure more from disgust with the nobility—for whom this was a very bad outcome—than from love of country. So strong was the animus that existed between the classes.

Fear descended on the rest. As the celebrations of the plebs and the defeat of his own party were happening, Marcus Scaurus, who as I stated above had been Bestia's deputy, engineered things during the public turbulence so that he would be named as one of the three investigators called for by Mamilius's bill. But the inquiry was done roughly and unreasonably, with a reliance on rumor and arbitrary passions. As had often happened for the nobles and this time occurred for the plebs: insolence followed in the wake of success.

XLI. The habits of partisanship, factionalism, and all related pernicious practices had arisen in Rome a few years before due to excessive leisure and the abundance of all things that mortal men

---

[166] Between the commons (plebs) and the nobles.

consider most important. Before Carthage was destroyed[167] the senate and the Roman people handled the political affairs of the republic peacefully and with discipline; rivalries among citizens for glory or domination did not exist. Fear of the external enemy kept the state focused on useful domestic endeavors. But when this fear lost its hold on the minds of the citizenry, unrestraint and arrogance inevitably grew, as these vices go hand-in-hand with opulence. Thus the leisure they hoped for during their hardships was in fact—after they had gotten it—more bitter and unkind than their original troubles. So the nobles abused their positions to indulge their vices, and the people abused their liberty to indulge their own; every man stole, plundered, and robbed for himself. Thus everything was pulled forcibly to two extremes; and the republic, which was caught in the middle, was torn apart.

The nobility was able to exert factional power to a greater degree. The power of the plebs, dissolute and dispersed as it was among the multitude, was less. The decisions of a few determined questions of war and domestic policy; in these same hands were the treasury, the control of the provinces, the civil offices, and the opportunities for glory and triumphs.[168] The populace was weighed down by military service and poverty. Generals appropriated the spoils of war with a few cronies. Meanwhile the parents or little children of soldiers were evicted from their houses if they had a more powerful neighbor.

Thus greed on the side of political power, without limit or restraint, infiltrated, polluted, and destroyed everything. It cared about nothing and held nothing sacred until the very moment it

---

[167] Carthage was destroyed in 146 B.C.

[168] It appears Sallust means (*gloriae triumphique*) the opportunity for public recognition of military prowess in the form of triumphs (i.e., parades) and glory (public honor).

destroyed itself. For as soon as nobles who valued true glory[169] more than unjust authority appeared, the political order was undermined, and civil strife broke out like a convulsion of the earth.

XLII. After Tiberius and Caius Gracchus, whose ancestors gave so much in service of the republic during the Punic and other wars,[170] began to champion the legal rights of the plebs and reveal the crimes of the wealthy elites, the guilty nobility was dismayed. They put obstacles in the way of the reforms of the Gracchi: they used the allies and the Latin communities of Italy, as well as the Roman knights, who distanced themselves from the plebs out of hope of an alliance with the nobility. First Tiberius was killed violently; then a few years later his brother Caius, who had taken up the same cause, met the same fate. One was a tribune and the other a commissioner for colonies.[171] Marcus Fulvius Flaccus was killed along with them.[172] It must be said, however, that the spirit of the Gracchi—with its lust for victory—was insufficiently moderate. But a good man would prefer to be defeated rather than eradicate injustice through evil conduct.[173]

Through this victory the nobility indulged its wantonness; it destroyed many opponents with violence or forced exile; but rather than augment its power, these acts only made it even more

---

[169] By "true glory" is meant "just rule" or "responsible conduct."

[170] The Gracchi came from a politically connected family. Tiberius's maternal grandparent was Publius Cornelius Scipio Africanus (i.e., the Elder), and his sister Sempronia was the wife of Publius Cornelius Scipio Aemilianus.

[171] Tiberius was the tribune of the plebs and Caius the *triumvirum coloniis deducundis.*

[172] Flaccus was an ally of the Gracchi. He was elected consul in 125 B.C. but was killed while leading a demonstration in 121 B.C. on the Aventine Hill.

[173] Meaning that the Gracchi, as good men, decided not to adopt the evil tactics of the nobility: *Sed bono vinci satius est quam malo more iniuriam vincere.*

feared. This behavior has led to the ruin of many great nations: when one faction defeats another by whatever means it can and lusts to punish the defeated with undue harshness. But if I were to furnish here a study of factionalism and of Rome's entire political scene, either in detail or as part of a more general analysis, time would desert me sooner than my history would be completed.[174] For this reason I will now return to my undertaking.

XLIII. After the signing of Aulus's treaty and our army's disgraceful flight,[175] the consuls elect Metellus and Silanus divided up the provinces between themselves. Numidia went to Metellus, a man of keen intelligence; although he was aligned against the popular party, his reputation nevertheless was steady and unblemished. When he first began his term of office, he readied his mind for the war he was about to wage, believing that he shared with his colleague all other official duties. Lacking confidence in the regular army's veterans, he called up recruits, sent for reinforcements from different places, and prepared equipment, weapons, and other instruments of war along with support materials: he collected everything, in fact, that would be needed for an irregular war[176] with extensive logistical requirements.

In making these preparations he was helped by the authority of the senate and by the voluntary sending of supplemental military units by allies, Latin communities, and kings.[177] The

---

[174] Sallust's purpose here is to give the reader some context that would explain the social and political factionalism that existed in Rome during the later republican period. He experienced it himself and obviously has strong feelings on the subject.

[175] There is a nice pun here that makes use of the dual meaning of the word *foedus*, which can mean either "treaty" or "flight": *post Auli foedus exercitusque nostri foedam fugam…*

[176] "Irregular war" is my preferred rendering of *bello vario*.

[177] It is not clear what foreign "kings" Sallust is referring to. Perhaps these were local rulers in the Balkans or Iberia.

entire state exerted the utmost effort. When everything had been prepared and arranged according to the requirements of his mission, Metellus set out for Numidia. He carried with him the high hopes of the citizenry; not only because of his good character traits, but even more because his mind could retain its integrity when faced with the temptation posed by riches. For it was the greed of the magistrates before this time that had ruined our efforts in Numidia and had helped those of the enemy.

XLIV. But when Metellus arrived in Africa, the army he received from the proconsul Spurius Albinus was demoralized, unfit for duty, and able to endure neither danger nor hardship; it was quicker with the tongue than with the sword-hand, a parasite on our allies while itself an easy target for the enemy, and subject to no leadership or discipline. Thus the new commander felt more anxiety from the unacceptable behavior of his soldiers than he felt reassurance or optimism from their numbers. Although the delay of the elections had impeded the summer season,[178] and Metellus knew the people of Rome looked forward to his victory, he still decided not to begin military operations until he had first forced the soldiers to drill with the discipline of their ancestors. Albinus, devastated by the defeat of his brother Aulus and the army, had resolved not to leave the province. During the time of summer when he was in command, he had essentially confined the soldiers to a permanent camp, except when unwholesome smells or the need for food for the animals compelled a change of location.

But the camp was not properly armed, and watches were not kept in accordance with military discipline; men would desert their posts whenever inclined to do so. Camp followers fraternizing with soldiers roamed around day and night; in these excursions they plundered farmlands, robbed houses, and competed with each other in collecting cattle and slaves as prizes.

---

[178]The summer season would be a time for conducting military operations.

These things they exchanged for foreign wines and other goods from merchants. They finally even sold the grain rations that the Roman government provided them and bartered for their bread from day to day. Whatever disgraces born of laziness and easy living that can be described or imagined—as well as a few others—could be found in this army.

XLV. But in this difficult situation—no less than in combat operations—I find Metellus to have been a great and judicious man: he prudently balanced a desire for popularity with the need for stern discipline. For as a first step he removed enablers of laziness with a command directive that no one could sell bread or other cooked food in the camp; that camp followers could not leech off the army; and that no common soldier could have a slave or mule with him in camp or on the march. He laid down strict rules for other things.

In addition he moved camp every day with extended marches and—just as if an enemy were near—fortified it with palisaded rampart and moat. He put in place regular watches and personally inspected them with his adjutants. When his forces were on the march he was sometimes at the head of the column, sometimes at the tail end, and often in the middle, to make sure that no stragglers dropped out of formation, that they marched as a cohesive unit under the standards, and that the soldiers properly carried their rations and weapons.[179] By removing the temptations for bad conduct rather than by punishing it, he restored his army's combat effectiveness in a short time.

XLVI. Meanwhile Jugurtha, who learned what Metellus was doing from his spies, also heard from Rome about his adversary's

---

[179] What Sallust is describing here is precisely what a modern military commander would do in "whipping into shape" a demoralized military unit. Based on this translator's experience, such techniques are extremely effective in restoring good discipline.

reputation for integrity. He grew uncertain about his plans and for the first time pondered making an actual surrender. He therefore sent emissaries to the consul with symbols of his desire to make peace;[180] he sought guarantees for his own life and the lives of his children, and left the rest to the will of the Roman people. But Metellus had learned from previous encounters that the people of Numidia were not the type to honor agreements; possessing volatile temperaments, they were always grasping for some new advantage. For this reason he made sure to separate the emissaries so he could interview them individually. After realizing they could be useful, he convinced them through personal guarantees to hand over Jugurtha: alive if possible, dead if not. Publicly, of course, he ordered them to report back to the king those things that were in alignment with the king's purposes.

A few days after this Metellus moved his army—a display of force that was prepared for action—into Numidia. Rather than finding evidence of a war, he saw dwellings filled with men and livestock and farmers in the fields. From the towns and native African communities the king's representatives greeted him, ready to provide grain, carry logistical supplies, and finally to do whatever they were ordered. Nevertheless Metellus advanced with his formations ready for action as if the enemy were all around them; he conducted long-range reconnaissance everywhere. He believed that these apparent signs of surrender were only for show and that the enemy was probing for an opportunity to ambush him.

At the head of the column was Metellus himself with the lightly-armed cohorts and a hand-picked group of slingers and archers; his deputy Caius Marius with the cavalry was responsible

---

[180] These *suppliciis* (symbols of submission) might have been gifts for Metellus, olive branches, or other similar tokens.

for the rear. On each side of the formation he assigned the cavalry of the auxiliaries to the tribunes of the legions and the prefects of the cohorts. Skirmishers[181] were mixed in with these men: their task was to defend against the assaults of enemy cavalry from wherever they might come. For Jugurtha was so cunning, so knowledgeable of the terrain and of military tactics, that it was uncertain whether he was more formidable when present or absent, during peacetime or when waging war.

XLVII. Not far from Metellus's route of ingress into Numidia was the Numidian town of Vaga, a well-known commercial hub of the entire kingdom where many men of Italic origin lived and engaged in business activities. Here the consul established a fortification, both to see if the inhabitants would tolerate it by showing goodwill, and because of the military expediency of the location.[182] He meanwhile directed his men to collect grain and other supplies used for war; as the situation indicated, he calculated that the large population of traders would assist in provisioning his army. It would also help safeguard the supplies he had already set aside.

While these events were happening, Jugurtha sent obsequious envoys with even more urgency: he begged stridently for peace and offered Metellus everything except his own life and the lives of his children. And just like the previous emissaries, the consul turned them to his purposes and sent them home; he neither promised nor refused the king the peace he proposed. Through

---

[181] The word used is *velites*, which can mean skirmishers, irregulars, or lightly-armed foot soldiers. The context seems to indicate that these were irregulars added to Metellus's column in a supporting role, but this is not certain.

[182] The text reads *ob opportunitates loci praesidium imposuit*. The context makes it clear that Metellus found Vaga a good place for a *praesidium* due to considerations of safety (the large Italic population made the town a friendly one) and from military necessity (it was on his line of march).

such delaying tactics Metellus waited for the envoys to do what he had instructed.

XLVIII. When Jugurtha compared Metellus's proclamations with his deeds, he came to understand that he was being played with his own tricks: peace was being dangled out with his adversary's words but in reality the harshest kind of war was underway. The king no longer controlled his most important city, the enemy was acquainted with his country's terrain, and the minds of his people were being tempted against him. The dictates of necessity ruled that he should seek battle. Therefore, after studying the enemy's route of ingress, he placed hopes of victory in the advantages offered by the terrain; he prepared the largest possible troop concentrations of all types and got in front of Metellus's army using hidden footpaths.

In this part of Numidia (which Adherbal had possessed after the initial division of the country) there was a river originating from the south called the Muthul. About twenty miles[183] from this was a cluster of mountains—barren of natural vegetation and human cultivation—that ran parallel with the Muthul. From about the middle of this cluster an elevation arose and stretched a long way in the distance; it was covered with olive, myrtle, and other types of trees able to sustain themselves in the arid and sandy soil. The middle plain[184] was uninhabited (except for places along the river) due to its lack of water; these riverside spots were thickly covered with small trees and were visited often by cattle and itinerant farmers.

XLIX. On this elevation—which extended across Metellus's line of march[185] as I have described—Jugurtha lay in wait with

---

[183] *Milia passuum viginti.* The Roman mile (*mille passus*) consisted of one thousand paces (counted by every other step).

[184] The twenty mile stretch of ground between the Muthul and the mountains.

[185] The phrase *transvorso itinere* is used, meaning that the elevation lay at a right angle across Metellus's line of march into Numidia.

his battle-line stretched out. He placed Bomilcar in command of the elephants and part of the infantry units and explained to him what he was going to do. He positioned his own men closer to the mountain with all the cavalry forces and his specially-selected infantry. Then visiting all his squadrons and companies individually he reminded them of, and sought to inspire them with, their ancient virtue and military victories; he implored them to defend themselves and their kingdom from Roman avarice. Jugurtha told them they would be in battle against men whom they had previously sent defeated under the yoke;[186] and that although the Roman commander had changed, the Roman morale had not.

Everything a field commander should give his men, he said, he had provided. They held the high ground where skilled fighters could overwhelm an enemy unfamiliar with the location; they were not a small number matched against a larger force, nor were they untrained men trying to fight battle-hardened soldiers. They must, therefore, be ready and willing to ambush the Romans when the signal was given. That day would either secure all their past labors and victories or would mark the beginning of the most terrible disasters. He reminded each soldier individually of the rewards of money or honor that had come to each of them while in the military; he pointed out such men to their fellow soldiers.[187] Finally through the use of promises, threats and exhortations according to each man's personality, he motivated his men in one way or another.

Meanwhile Metellus, ignorant of the enemy's presence, spotted them while descending the mountain with his army. At first the Romans were not sure what they were seeing, for the Numidians and their horses had situated themselves among the brushwood. They were not completely hidden due to the

---

[186] Referring to the defeat inflicted on Metellus's predecessor Aulus.

[187] A clever tactic to make sure his men knew they were indebted to him.

smallness of the shrubbery; yet it was not clear to the Romans what they faced, since Jugurtha's men and their military standards were obscured both by camouflage and by the terrain features. But Metellus quickly understood that it was an ambush and halted his column. He changed the composition of his right flank (which was nearest the enemy), fortifying it with three lines of reserve troops. He distributed slingers and archers between the maniples, and on the wings he placed all the cavalry. Using the brief time available he encouraged his soldiers; then he led his force down into the plain as he had organized it, with the head of the formation now acting as the flank.

L. But when he noticed that the Numidians stayed calm and did not move off the hill, he feared that because of the current season and the lack of water his army might be afflicted by thirst. He therefore sent ahead his officer Rutilius (with some lightly-armed cohorts and a unit of cavalry) to the river in order to seize some ground for a camp, thinking that the enemy would try to block his advance by repeated attacks on his flanks. He believed that because the Numidians lacked confidence in their battle skills, they would try to bring exhaustion and thirst to bear on his men. After surveying the situation and terrain, he finally moved forward little by little (just as he had descended from the mountain); Marius was placed behind the foremost ranks while Metellus was on the left wing with the cavalry, which had now become the leading part of the formation.

But when Jugurtha saw that the tail-end of Metellus's formation had marched past the foremost rank of his own force, he sent a detachment of about two thousand infantry to the mountain that Metellus had just moved away from, so that if the Romans were to withdraw, they would not have this area as a refuge behind them. Finally giving the signal, he attacked the Romans without warning. Some of the Numidians killed the men at the rear of Metellus's army, while others tried to attack the left and right flanks; furious fighting took place at close quarters and the Roman ranks in every sector were thrown into confusion. Even those who kept their morale high after being directly exposed to the enemy were not used to this kind of irregular warfare in which they could be wounded from a distance, being able neither to respond in kind nor fight their adversary face-to-face.[188]

As Jugurtha had previously taught his cavalry, they withdrew when a squadron of Romans attacked them: not in formation or as a cohesive unit, but in a greatly diffused way in multiple directions. Thus even if they could not prevent the enemy's pursuit, they could with their numerical advantage still surround Roman soldiers separated from their units at the rear and flanks of the formation. If the hill rather than the level ground had been a more advantageous place to retreat, the Numidians' horses—practiced at moving over such terrain—easily escaped by this route through the brushwood. But the harshness and unfamiliarity of the ground impeded the mobility of our own men.

LI. As a whole the character of the melee was mixed, uncertain, terrible, and tragic. As the Romans were scattered about, some were routed and others pursued the enemy. They neither followed the standards nor kept their formations intact; but when each soldier was confronted by danger, he fought back and repelled the foe. Together were jumbled close-quarters weapons and equipment, horses and men, Numidians and Romans. Neither battle-orders nor plans were given; fortune ruled everywhere.[189]

So passed most of the day; but the outcome was still in doubt. Finally, in the midst of all the physical activity and the sluggishness produced by the desert furnace, Metellus—when he saw that the Numidians were pressing him less intensely—

---

[188] The cadence of the word-play is very nice in the last part of the sentence: *neque contra feriundi aut conserundi manum copia erat.*
[189] Meaning that chance determined the outcome.

gradually brought his soldiers together into a coherent formation. He restored the integrity of the ranks and positioned four cohorts of legionaries to face the enemy's infantry, the greater part of which was exhausted and had retired to elevated terrain. At the same time he exhorted and pleaded with his men neither to falter nor permit the withdrawing enemy to outlast them. They had, he told his men, neither a camp nor any protective emplacement into which they could withdraw: everything now came down to their own arms. Meanwhile Jugurtha was not idle either: he roamed the battleground, exhorting his men and spurring on the fighting. By himself and with his elite soldiers he tried everything, gave his men assistance, and pursued the enemy at their weak points; he held at bay those enemy units perceived as strong by hitting them from a distance.

LII. In such fashion did these two commanders contend with each other as great men. Equal as individuals, they were otherwise disparate in resources. Metellus's men had good fighting ability but were stuck on unfavorable ground; Jugurtha had every other advantage except the relative quality of his men. Finally, when the Romans realized that there was no secure area for them to go to, that the enemy no longer was willing to engage them, and that it was already dusk, they escaped up the hill in accordance with their commander's intent. From this place the Numidians were expelled, routed, and put to flight. A few were slain; but their adversary's ignorance of the area combined with their own speed of maneuver rescued the majority.

Meanwhile Bomilcar, who as we noted above had been assigned command of the elephants and a part of the infantry by Jugurtha, little by little guided his forces down to level ground[190] after Rutilius moved passed him. Rutilius proceeded to move quickly towards the river (the place to which he had been sent);

---

[190] From the high ground to the plain.

without making noise Bomilcar made ready his battle line as the situation dictated. He never stopped monitoring what the Romans were doing across the entire battlefield.

Once he realized that Rutilius had halted and let down his guard somewhat—and at the same time the roar of battle from Jugurtha's sector grew louder—he worried that the deputy,[191] once aware of his comrades' predicament, would go to help them. Lacking confidence in his unit's battle discipline, Bomilcar drew up his ranks in tight formation;[192] he stretched out his line in order to block the enemy's direction of movement and in this posture headed towards Rutilius's camp.

LIII. Suddenly the Romans noticed a huge veil of dust, for the heavy vegetation hindered their ability to see things clearly. They first thought it was dry dirt kicked up by the wind; but when they saw that the cloud preserved its shape and continued to move closer and closer by degrees, they finally realized what it was. Quickly taking up their arms, they moved into position in front of the camp as commanded. When the enemy finally came near enough, both sides ran to meet each other with a huge roar. The Numidians kept their formation as long as they thought their elephants were helping them; but when the animals became ensnared in tree-branches and then scattered and surrounded, their masters made their escape. Most of them threw down their weapons and, making use of the hill and the approaching night, got away with their lives. Four elephants were captured; the entire remainder—which totaled forty—were killed.

Although the Romans were exhausted by the march, the work on the camp, and the battle, they nevertheless advanced to meet Metellus (who had been delayed longer than expected) in battle formation and at the ready. For the guile of the Numidians could

---

[191] Meaning Rutilius (*legatus* means deputy or lieutenant).
[192] In close quarters so that they could be controlled more easily.

permit neither inattention nor laxity. At this point it was completely dark and the two units were not far from each other. The noise generated as the two forces drew near, one upon the other, struck both fear and confusion in the ranks. A miscalculation could have spelled total disaster had not mounted riders on both sides conducted reconnaissance along the line of contact between the two forces.[193] Fear was unexpectedly transformed into elation. The ecstatic soldiers yelled out to each other and chattered about what they had done and heard; each man embellished his own deeds to the heavens. Human affairs naturally have this quality: the craven may boast in times of victory, but failure vilifies even the valiant.

LIV. Metellus stayed in the same camp for a period of four days to provide care for the wounded. He handed out decorations for good conduct during the battle, complimented and thanked all the men as a whole, and called on them to handle the lighter remaining tasks with the same forceful spirit. There had been enough fighting to produce victory; their remaining labors would be for plunder. Nevertheless, in the meantime, he sent enemy deserters and other available intelligence assets to find out where Jugurtha was, what he was doing, whether he had only a few men left with him or still possessed an army, and how he was handling himself in defeat.

In fact he had retreated to a naturally fortified wooded area; and there he was in the process of collecting together an army of even greater size, but weaker and less professional, as his conscripts were more familiar with animal husbandry and farming than military matters. This was because no Numidian soldier follows his king in flight after a defeat except his personal cavalry

---

[193] I have opted for a modern military term ("line of ground contact") that fits best the gist of Sallust's vague wording (*praemissi equites rem exploravissent*) on the disposition of forces.

guard. They drift off wherever they wish to go, and this is not considered a soldierly disgrace. It is simply their custom.

When Metellus saw that the king's mind was still set on fighting, and that the war would be continued only as Jugurtha's pleasure dictated, he resolved to prosecute the campaign not by conventional warfare tactics but in a very different way.[194] The contest with the enemy was decidedly a disadvantageous one: for it cost the enemy less to be defeated than it cost Metellus to defeat them. He therefore moved into the most well-resourced part of Numidia to ravage its agricultural lands, seized and burned many fortified positions and towns that were inadequately protected or lacked garrisons, ordered adult males to be slain, and distributed everything else to his soldiers as plunder. By means of such terror tactics many natives were handed over to the Romans as hostages,[195] grain and other supplies that could be used were plentifully given, and garrisons were established wherever Metellus requested.

These tactics frightened the king much more than the previous battle that had gone badly for him. For while he had placed all his hopes in making use of hit-and-run tactics, he was forced to follow around his opponent; when he was deprived of the ability to

---

[194] A key sentence pointing to the decision to move from conventional war (*proeliis in acie*) to war "by other means" (*alio more*). Jugurtha's ability to field numerically superior forces meant that he would eventually be able to grind down Metellus unless the Roman commander adopted different tactics.
[195] Native hostages (*obsides*) could be useful as a form of collateral or security to ensure that agreements were honored. Julius Caesar would use this tactic artfully—and ruthlessly—in his Gallic campaign. According to one writer, hostages acted as sureties in situations involving "exchange, unilateral exaction by formal national agreement, private contract, and extralegal seizure." *See* Walker, Cheryl, *Hostages in Republican Rome*, "Chapter 1: Meaning and Purpose of Hostageship in the Greco-Roman World" [1-20], http://chs.harvard.edu/publications.

conduct defensive operations in his own areas, he had to carry on the fight in other places.[196] Nevertheless he made use of the plans that seemed best for his forces. He ordered the majority of his army to wait in the same place while he himself set out with the elite cavalry to chase Metellus. At night and though obscure pathways, he ambushed small Roman units that were unprepared. A great many of them were killed without their weapons; a good number were captured; and no one got away unharmed. Before relief could arrive from the Roman camp, the Numidians would withdraw to the closest hills, just as they had been ordered.

LV. Meanwhile at Rome a great deal of fanfare arose at the knowledge of Metellus's deeds and the public learned he had behaved—and had led his army—in a way befitting our ancestors. Through his own virtue he had emerged from a very difficult position as the victor. He was occupying the enemy's territory and forcing Jugurtha, empowered by Albinus's inaction, to place his hopes on either exile in the wilderness or flight. The senate, therefore, passed a resolution of gratitude to the immortal gods for these developments; the citizenry, previously edgy and nervous about the outcome of the war, now responded with celebration. Metellus's public stature soared. He therefore pressed even more strenuously for victory, staying busy in every way: yet he took care not to provide the enemy an opportunity anywhere, mindful of the fact that jealousy follows in the wake of glory.

Thus the more notoriety he received, the more careful he became. After Jugurtha's ambush Metellus no longer plundered

---

[196] This important sentence encapsulates the essence of counterinsurgency operations. Previous translations have not rendered Sallust's words in this paragraph and the next in a way that conveys this point adequately. Modern military terminology is needed and I have opted for it here. Metellus's strategy throws Jugurtha off his game and takes the initiative away from him. Instead of chasing Jugurtha around, he forces the Numidian to chase *him* around.

the countryside with his army somewhat disheveled; when he needed grain or animal fodder, several cohorts and all the cavalry were posted as security. He led part of the army himself and delegated the remainder to Marius. But the countryside was laid waste more by fires than by looting. They set up camp in two places not far apart from each other. When combat strength was needed they merged together; at other times they operated separately so that the enemy's fear and desire to flee would expand over a greater area.

During this time Jugurtha would track them along the hills, looking for the right opportunity and place to fight. In the places where he had heard the Romans would be coming, he destroyed the fodder and poisoned the wells (which were quite scarce). He revealed himself at one time to Metellus, and to Marius at another; he harassed the end of the Roman line and then immediately withdrew to the hills. He threatened some units and then again others, neither joining in battle nor permitting the foe to lower its guard: by such methods he frustrated the enemy's goals.

LVI. When the Roman commander saw that he was being worn down by this guile that provided no chance to confront the other side's conventional forces, he decided to attack Zama, one of the kingdom's strongholds in the area. He believed this move would create a situation where Jugurtha would come to the aid of his beleaguered comrades, and that a decisive battle could then take place. But Jugurtha, having learned from Roman deserters what was being prepared, arrived before Metellus by covering great distances on the march. He called on the townspeople to defend their walls and assigned Roman deserters to help them. These deserters—who could never think of betraying him—were the most robust group of all the king's forces.[197] He also promised

---

[197] Reliable in the sense that they knew their lives would be forfeit if Jugurtha

that he would come with an army at the appropriate time. After drawing up these plans he withdrew to an undisclosed location; a little bit later he learned that Marius had been diverted from his route to look for food at Sicca[198] with the help of a few cohorts. It was one of the very first towns to defect from the king after his unlucky battle.

Jugurtha made his way to this town with a select group of cavalry and attacked the Romans at the gates as they were coming out; at the same time he called out loudly to the inhabitants of Sicca to encircle the cohorts on the far side. Fortune had offered them the chance for a memorable deed. If they were able to do this—he exhorted them—they would from that time be able to live their lives without fear and in freedom. And if Marius had not carried the standard[199] and moved quickly to escape the town, surely all or a large part of the Siccans would have switched their loyalties. With such capriciousness do the Numidians conduct themselves. For a time Jugurtha's soldiers stood their ground with his help, but eventually the foreigners hammered them with greater force, and they withdrew in flight with mild casualties.

LVII. Marius continued to Zama. The city was located on a plain and protected more by man-made defenses than by its inherent location; it was deficient in no essential resource and contained more than enough arms and men. Metellus therefore planned his operation with a careful eye to the situation and the terrain; he surrounded the entire length of the city's walls with his army and ordered each of his commanders to focus on a specific sector. Finally the signal was given. All at once a huge roar arose from every side, but this did not rattle the Numidians; keeping

---

ever sent them back to the Romans.

[198] The location of Sicca was apparently on the banks of the Bagradas. A noted temple of Venus stood there. *See* Valerius Maximus II.6.

[199] Carrying the Roman battle standard (*signa inferre*) would have meant "leading from the front" or rallying the men to go forward.

their composure, they maintained a grim resolution and bristled with combativeness. The battle then began. Each Roman fought according to his own talent: some used slings or missiles hurled from a distance; some pushed close to the walls and tried to weaken them by digging; others raised ladders to grapple with the enemy in hand-to-hand fighting. To counteract these tactics the inhabitants rolled heavy stones onto the nearest attackers; they also threw logs, spears, flaming pitch mixed with sulphur,[200] and burning torches.

Even the caution of those who kept at a distance was not enough to protect them, for many were wounded by projectiles thrown by hand or launched by engines. Thus were the brave and the timid, though unequal in virtue, made equal through danger.

LVIII. While this battle was being fought at Zama, Jugurtha attacked the enemy's camp with a large force and, on account of the lackadaisical quality of the sentries there who were expecting anything but a major engagement, burst through the gates. Our soldiers were suddenly seized with panic. Each man reverted to his own individual nature:[201] some fled the scene, others reached for their arms, but the majority were killed or wounded. Out of the entire group no more than forty men preserved the Romans' good name. They formed a group and occupied a location a bit more elevated than its surroundings; from here they could not be driven off by the most intense enemy attacks. They hurled back the javelins that were thrown at them from a distance and, with so few contending against so many, it was hardly possible for their weapons to miss a target. But if the Numidians came closer, the Romans then showed their virtue[202] by striking them down with great force, scattering them, or putting them to flight.

---

[200] So old are the progenitors of the Byzantine "Greek fire."

[201] Meaning that they lost their military discipline and cohesion.

[202] *Ibi vero virtutem ostendere.* Sallust's concept of virtue is one of the keystones of his worldview.

Meanwhile Metellus, completely absorbed in his own fight, heard the clamor of an enemy behind his position. Turning around his horse, he observed men in flight coming towards him: this told him they were his own people. He therefore quickly sent all the cavalry to the camp and told Caius Marius immediately to go there as well. With tears in his eyes Metellus begged Marius, in the name of their comradeship and the republic, not to permit some disgrace to tarnish the good name of his victorious army and not to let the enemy get away unscathed. Marius quickly carried out the order.

Jugurtha, meanwhile, was impeded by the camp's defenses. Some of his men were being thrown off the ramparts while others trying to do their jobs in the crowded sectors were getting in each other's ways. He withdrew to a protected area after sustaining a large number of casualties. His work left incomplete, Metellus returned to camp with his army after nightfall.

LIX. So the next day, before going out to continue the struggle, Metellus ordered his entire cavalry to conduct reconnaissance in the area around the camp where Jugurtha had made incursions; to the tribunes he delegated the security of the gates and the sectors adjoining them. Finally he advanced on the town and launched an attack on the walls as on the previous day. Meanwhile, Jugurtha at once attacked our men from a concealed location. Those nearest the line of engagement were for a short time thrown into shock, but the rest of their comrades quickly came to their aid. The Numidians would not long have been able to withstand the pressure had not their infantry, operating in a coordinated manner with their cavalry, caused great devastation during the melee. Relying on the infantry, their cavalry did not advance and then withdraw as horsemen are accustomed to do in battle, but rather struck at the Roman battle-line directly, folding it on itself and causing mayhem. Thus they nearly defeated their enemy using light infantry.

LX. The fighting continued at Zama with great intensity during this same time. Wherever each of the tribunes or deputies

168

was in command, there occurred the most brutal combat; no man placed more trust in his comrade than in himself. The inhabitants of the town practiced the same ethic; in every sector of the battle-zone they either fought or made preparations for fighting. Each belligerent was more obsessed with hurting its opponent than with protecting itself. The epic roar of battle was mixed with exhortations, hysterical cries of joy, and groans of lamentation; the sound of the frenzied clash of arms was carried aloft to the sky; and javelins flew from every direction.

But whenever the Romans suspended their assault for even a short time, the men defending the walls watched the cavalry battle with great interest. Whatever situation Jugurtha's cavalry found itself in, you could see the spectators perched on the walls ecstatic one minute and panic-stricken the next. Just as if the horsemen were able to see or hear them, some called out warnings and others shouted encouragement; they waved their arms and twisted their bodies this way and that as if they were taking evasive action or throwing javelins.

When Marius became aware of this—he was by this time in command of this sector—he deliberately eased up the pressure on the enemy and pretended to be wavering in his resolution in order to allow the Numidans to watch their king's cavalry battle without distraction. While the defenders were transfixed by watching this spectacle, he suddenly launched an attack on the wall with tremendous force. Clambering up raised ladders the Roman attackers almost reached the top of the wall; but the defenders ran to engage them, hurling heavy stones, flaming materials, and all kinds of flying weapons. Our men tried to fight back at first. But when one ladder after another was smashed, and the men standing on them were thrown headlong to the ground, their comrades withdrew in whatever way was available. The majority of the men were seriously wounded, although a few were uninjured. Nightfall finally brought an end to the fighting for both sides.

LXI. Once Metellus could see that his undertaking was futile, that the town had neither been captured nor would Jugurtha fight except with hit-and-run tactics or at places of his own choosing, and that the summer season was ending, he withdrew from Zama and set up garrisons in those towns that had defected to him and were sufficiently protected by natural terrain or by walls. The rest of the army he positioned for the winter season in the Roman province closest to Numidia. But he did not spend this time—as others often do—in rest or luxury. Since the war was not going very well from a military standpoint, he would now experiment with treachery by enlisting the king's associates: he would use their perfidy as weapons.

He therefore sought out Bomilcar, who had been at Rome with Jugurtha and—once he was granted bail—became a fugitive to avoid trial for the murder of Massiva. Because Bomilcar's close relationship with Jugurtha provided ideal opportunities for duping the king, Metellus aimed to win him over with a variety of promises. His first scheme was to represent that Jugurtha should visit him secretly for truce talks. If Jugurtha were delivered into Metellus's custody dead or alive, the senate (on the Roman commander's personal guarantee) would grant him and all his property immunity from prosecution and forfeiture. The Numidian was easily seduced by this, as his character was shifty by nature. He was also worried that if peace with Rome came, one of its terms would be that he himself would be handed over for punishment.

LXII. At the first available opportunity—when Jugurtha was feeling apprehension and self-pity about his fortunes—Bomilcar made contact with him. He counseled the king and implored him tearfully that he should make arrangements for himself, his children, and the Numidian people who deserved so much. He pointed out that they had been defeated in many battles, their agricultural lands had been stripped clean, they had lost a great number of men through death or capture, and the kingdom's productive capacity had been shattered. He had put both his soldiers' virtue and fortune itself to the test long enough, Bomilcar said. He warned him that if he were slow to act on these present realities, the Numidian people would do his thinking for him.[203] By raising these points—and others like them—he gently pushed the king towards consideration of a negotiated surrender.

Peace envoys were sent to the Roman commander to say that Jugurtha would do as he was told; he would place his kingdom and himself personally in Metellus's hands without any formal agreement. The general immediately mobilized from their winter billets all men from the senatorial class; he then convened a meeting with them and a few others judged to be suitable. In accordance with the decision of this conference (which was mindful of our ancestral custom), Metellus told Jugurtha's envoys that the king must deliver to him two hundred thousand pounds of silver, all his elephants, and significant numbers of weapons and horses. After these terms were complied with, he directed Jugurtha to hand over all Roman military deserters in chains. Most of them were given to Metellus as ordered, but some had absconded to King Bocchus in Mauretania[204] once peace negotiations started.

Thus Jugurtha—now deprived of his men, arms, and money— was himself ordered to appear at Tisidium.[205] But he once again began to lose his nerve, fearful of facing justice on account of his guilty conscience. Finally, after spending many days in fitful vacillation, on the one hand so exhausted with his troubles as to consider anything better than more war, and at the same time

---

[203] I.e., that they would draw their own conclusions on the state of the war and rebel against him.

[204] Bocchus I of Mauretania ruled from about 110 B.C. to 85 B.C. Precise dates are not available. He was also Jugurtha's father-in-law.

[205] The location of this town is not certain. It may be the same destroyed town mentioned in Strabo XVII.

reflecting on how horrific a reversal it was for him to go from king to prisoner of war after losing so much wealth and so many men to absolutely no avail, he chose to renew the war. At Rome the senate deliberated on some questions related to the provinces and assigned Numidia to Metellus.

LXIII. By chance at the same time at Utica a diviner[206] uttered an extraordinary and momentous prophecy when Caius Marius was sacrificing some animals to the gods: the soothsayer told Marius that he should listen to his inner spirit and conduct himself with trust in the gods; he should put fortune to the test as often as he could with the knowledge that all his enterprises would turn out favorably. Even before this Marius had been stirred by a fervent desire for the Roman consulship, for which he possessed all the necessary qualities except a patrician family. He had industry, honesty, extensive knowledge of military affairs, and a spirit remarkable in war but restrained in civilian life; he was in firm control of his passions and free from avarice, and passionate only for glory.

He was born in Arpinum[207] and had spent his youth there. When he first reached the age where his body could tolerate army life he entered military service; he did not chase after Greek eloquence or the refinements of city life. By applying himself to worthy arts he quickly reached manhood with a robust character. Thus when he first sought the office of military tribune from the people, he was elected unanimously by all the tribes; many people did not know what he looked like but his deeds were held in high regard. After this he acquired one public office after another, always handling his authority in such a way as to be seen worthy of a higher office than the one he currently occupied. Although

---

[206] A *haruspex* was a trained soothsayer who could "read" the entrails of sacrificed animals for predictions of present and future events. According to the Oxford Latin Dictionary their class originated in Etruria.

[207] Modern Arpino, a city in central Italy in the province of Frosinone.

later he became enslaved by ambition, nevertheless at this time he was such a good man that he dared not seek the consulship. The plebs could grant other civil offices, but the consulship was passed among members of the nobility from hand to hand. No "new man" was so exceptional or so renowned for his accomplishments that he could be considered worthy of this honor and not somehow "tainted."[208]

LXIV. Therefore when Marius saw that the diviner's pronouncements illuminated the same destination to which his secret cravings were guiding him, he asked Metellus for a leave absence to pursue his ambition.[209] Although Metellus excelled in masculine virtue, martial glory, and other qualities desired by good men, he nevertheless carried with him a certain hauteur and conceit, personal deficiencies commonly encountered in the nobility. He was at first shocked by Marius's bizarre request, then dismayed by his political ambitions; pretending to advise him as a friend, he warned Marius not to embark on such an ill-advised project or to pursue a goal that fate never intended for him.[210] He told him that not everyone should covet everything, and that he ought to be content with what he already had. Metellus finally forewarned him not to demand from the Roman people something that they had every right to deny.

---

[208] "Tainted" in the sense of being "polluted" (*pollutus*) by coming from a non-noble family. Class distinctions were sharp in ancient Rome. A "new man" (*novus homo*) was someone who was the first in his family to be chosen for the senate or elected consul. Cicero was one such man; even more remarkable was the fact that he attained the consulship at a young age (43).

[209] To run for the office of consul.

[210] The last part of this sentence expresses a sentiment very Roman and not easily conveyed in English. *Neu super fortunam animum gereret* literally means "and he should not manage his spirit above its fate" or "he should not conduct himself above his fortune." The idea is of someone doing something "beyond his natural place" in life.

After Metellus made these and other similar points without changing Marius's mind, he finally told him he would do what he asked as soon the current military matters of state permitted. Later when Marius repeatedly submitted the same application, Metellus is supposed to have informed him that he should be in no hurry to go, and that he would be able to seek the consulship when Metellus's own son was old enough to do so.[211] At that time Metellus's son was about twenty years old and fulfilling his military obligation as a part of his father's headquarters element.[212] This incident stoked Marius's ambition for the consulship that much more and fueled an incendiary hatred against Metellus.

Marius prowled about, therefore, with the worst advisors at his side: Ambition and Rage. He abstained from no word or deed that would advance his personal program. He was more lax than he was before in maintaining the discipline of the soldiers billeted in their winter camps; he jabbered slanderously and braggingly to merchants in Utica (of which there were a great many) about the war.[213] If he were permitted to have half the present army's size, he said, he would have Jugurtha in chains in a few days. He also claimed that Metellus, as a conceited man possessed of regal arrogance, was deliberately dragging out the conflict because he relished too much the power of his command. Since the city merchants had seen their commercial profits dwindle from the

---

[211] Military veterans will read these lines with knowing smiles. The psychologies of field commanders towards subordinates have changed little since Sallust's day. It is never a good idea to request favors from one's commanding officer in the middle of a campaign.

[212] The age of forty-three was the minimum age at which a man could run for the consulship. The intent behind Metellus's snide comment is obvious.

[213] This was not only a serious security breach (merchants travel widely and talk to many) but a remarkable act of disloyalty from a subordinate officer in time of war.

war's long duration, all of Marius's backbiting was well-received by them. Nothing moves rapid enough for the avaricious heart.

LXV. There was in our army a Numidian named Gauda, a son of Mastanabal and grandson of Masinissa, whom Micipsa had named as a secondary beneficiary[214] in his will. He possessed a sickly constitution and for this reason his mental capacity was somewhat impaired. He requested from Metellus the privilege of royal honors in that he should be allowed to sit beside the commander; to this he later added the demand of personal protection by a squadron of Roman cavalry. Both of these requests were denied: royal honors, because they were appropriate only for those whom the Roman people officially recognized as kings; the personal protection squad, because it would be humiliating to have Roman knights to serve as courtiers to a Numidian.

Marius made contact with the rebuffed Gauda and emboldened him to seek revenge (with his help) on the general for his humiliation. With glowing language he praised this sick, feeble-minded man, telling him he was a king, a man of importance, and the grandson of Masinissa; and if Jugurtha were captured or killed, the Numidian throne would be his without delay. This could actually happen—he assured Gauda—if he himself were made consul and sent to war. Winning over some by his personal charisma and others by their desire for peace, Marius thus persuaded Gauda and the Roman knights (both soldiers and merchants) to write disparagingly about Metellus's handling of the war to their friends in Rome and to demand that Marius replace him as the commanding general. The end result was that many men backed his quest for the consulship with extremely favorable expressions of support. At just this moment the nobility

---

[214] A secondary legatee received an inheritance if the primary legatee was unable to do so through death or incapacity.

had suffered a defeat by the passing of the Mamilian law,[215] and the lower classes were beginning to favor "new men." Thus all the external factors were operating in Marius's favor.

LXVI. Meanwhile Jugurtha, setting aside the prospect of surrender to the Romans, was moving to renew the war. With great attention to detail he prepared his logistics as quickly as possible: he assembled an army, tried using bribery or threats to win back the cities that had defected from him, and strengthened the territory he already held. He manufactured or bought arms, weapons, and other items he had lost during the peace negotiations; he enticed the slaves of the Romans to turn against their masters, and even tried to bribe the soldiers manning the enemy fortifications. He experimented with every ruse, and allowed nothing to be untried or unexamined.

Thus the Vagenses, on whose territory Metellus had first placed a garrison during the peace talks with Jugurtha, submitted to the king's demands, never having lost their goodwill towards him. The town's notables then made a conspiratorial pact with him. The commoners—as is usually the case but especially true among Numidians—had a volatile character; seditious and inclined to revolt, they loved whatever was new and were uninterested in peace and quiet. After taking care of the preliminary arrangements among themselves, they set a date three days from that time;[216] the day was a popular holiday all over Africa during which public games and entertainments would be more on display than vigilance.

But when the time came, they invited the centurions, military tribunes, and the town's prefect himself Titus Turpilius Silanus to their various homes. All of them except Turpilius were murdered

---

[215] Discussed in section XL.
[216] On which date the town's leading citizens would implement the conspiracy.

176

during their meals. The plotters then attacked the regular soldiers, who were walking around without their weapons, as was normal on a day when they were at rest. The common rabble joined in the violence. Some were goaded on by the nobility; others were aroused by a lust for such behavior. Though they were ignorant of the meaning and purpose of the slaughter, the attraction of violent revolt and anarchy was enough to satisfy them.

LXVII. The Roman soldiers, disoriented by sudden panic and in doubt about what the best course of action was, wavered. The town's previously closed gates prevented their escape, and an enemy force blocked their access to the citadel (where their standards and weapons were). From the roofs of the houses, women and boys eagerly threw rocks and whatever else was available at them. It was impossible for a man to protect himself from both of these terrible scenarios; and the bravest could not fight back against the weakest of assailants. Side by side good men and bad, soldierly and peaceable, were cut down with impunity.

The town was completely closed and the Numidians were afire with rage; Turpilius (the prefect in command) escaped unharmed from this frightful carnage alone out of all the Italians. We do not know whether this was due to the compassion of his host, some secret agreement, or blind luck; nevertheless, because a shameful life after such a calamity was for him more important than maintaining his honor, he must be considered both immoral and contemptible.

LXVIII. After Metellus was made aware of the events at Vaga, he secluded himself to grieve in private. Finally, when his grief had fused together with anger, he began to make careful preparations for vengeance. At sunset he marched out the legion that was in winter quarters along with as many lightly-armed Numidian cavalrymen as were available; at about the third hour of the next day he reached a plain enclosed by more highly-elevated terrain features. Here he assured his soldiers—by now exhausted by the length of the march and ready to refuse orders to continue—that the town of Vaga was only a mile[217] away. They should endure the remaining labor with a stoic spirit, he told them, so that they could exact retribution for the sake of their valiant and unfortunate comrades. He also benevolently pointed out the plunder that would be available. Having thus girded their spines, he ordered the cavalry to advance first in a wide deployment; the infantry would follow them in tight ranks with their standards concealed.

LXIX. When the Vagenses observed that an army was marching towards them, they at once shut the city gates, believing (correctly) that it was Metellus. Eventually, when the surrounding agricultural lands were left untouched and they saw that the cavalrymen at the head of the army were Numidians, they reconsidered and believed it was Jugurtha. Swept away with delight, they ventured out into the open to greet him. The signal was given: all at once, infantry and cavalry fell upon the crowds streaming out from the town. Some units rushed towards the gates, others moved to seize the towers; rage and a lust for plunder entirely replaced their exhaustion.

And so for two days were the people of Vaga able to celebrate their duplicity; their great and opulent city then became the embodiment of revenge and depradation. The city's former prefect Turpilius, who as we explained earlier was the only man to have fled the city successfully, was ordered by Metellus to give an account of his actions. When his testimony was judged to be entirely inadequate, he was found guilty, flogged, and then—for he was only a Latin citizen—executed.[218]

---

[217] *Mille passuum*, the standard mile of a thousand paces.

[218] Meaning that he was not a Roman citizen, but a non-Roman Italian. Roman citizens were not subject to such severe punishments. We should note that Plutarch gives a quite different account of Turpilius's fate in the *Life of*

LXX. At the same time Bomilar, at whose prodding Jugurtha had begun the surrender talks that he later broke off out of anxiety, was both wary of the king and at the same time mistrusted by him; he was eager for regime change and hunted about for some device that might produce Jugurtha's downfall. These thoughts oppressed his mind day and night. Finally after considering everything else he secured the trust of one Nabdalsa, a nobleman of great resources, renowned and well-liked by his people. For the most part he controlled an armed force independent of the king and was used to tending to those matters that escaped Jugurtha's attention when he was tired or absorbed in more pressing concerns. Power and prominence had come to him by way of this arrangement. A joint plan was formed with Bomilcar and a day set for their treachery; they were content to handle things as they happened and as the situation required.

Nabdalsa went to the army, which he had been told to position between the Romans' winter camp[219] so that the surrounding lands would not be ravaged by the enemy with impunity. Once the magnitude of his actions began to dawn on him, he did not come

---

Marius, VIII. Turpilius may have been a victim of the power struggle between Metellus and Marius. Plutarch says that Turpilius had been popular among the Vagans for his mildness and good temper in governing the city. When the inhabitants let Jugurtha into Vaga, they wanted Turpilius spared and Jugurtha complied. In this version of events, it was Marius, and not Metellus, who thought Turpilius had behaved traitorously and insisted on his execution. Furthermore, Turpilius had been an old friend of Metellus's family. Marius overruled all the other members of the military tribunal (including Metellus, who wanted him spared) and ultimately had his way. This incident, according to Plutarch, was what set Marius and Metellus on terms of permanent hostility with each other.

[219] The "between" wording is somewhat vague but appears to mean that the army should shadow the Roman camp to prevent the enemy from plundering the countryside.

at the appointed time, crippled by fear. Bomilcar, eager to carry out their plan and at the same time worried his accomplice's unreliability would induce him to look for a new agreement after tossing out the old one, sent him a letter through secure couriers. He berated the man for his torpor and weakness, invoked the gods to whom Nabdalsa had sworn, and warned him not to transform Metellus's rewards into a curse.[220] He reminded him that Jugurtha's final hour was approaching; the only question was whether he would meet his end through Metellus's prowess or through their own. Hence he should seriously ask himself whether he preferred rewards or torture.

LXXI. When this letter was brought to Nabdalsa he was by chance reclining on his couch, his body worn out from training. His first reaction upon reading its contents was concern; eventually, as often happens when the mind is oppressed by thought, he dozed off. He had a Numidian personal assistant, loyal and very dear to him, who was a confidant in all of his projects except this most recent one. When this attendant heard that a letter had been delivered, he entered Nabdalsa's tent in accordance with his usual practice, believing that his help or counsel might be needed; discovering his master asleep with a letter foolishly placed beside his head on a pillow, he took it and read it. Immediately alerted to its treasonous contents, he reported it to the king.

Nabdalsa awoke shortly after this. When he was unable to locate the letter, the full implications of what had happened now dawned on him. He first tried to intercept his betrayer; when this was unsuccessful, he rushed to Jugurtha in an attempt to appease him. He characterized what he himself had plotted to do as the original contrivance of his personal assistant. Weeping, he

---

[220] By "Metellus's rewards" is meant the opportunities presented by his battlefield successes.

pleaded with the king in the name of their friendship and his record of devoted service not to suspect him of such wrongdoing.

LXXII. To this display the king responded mildly, although his true sentiments were quite different. After executing Bomilcar and many others he knew were complicit in the plot, he brought his anger under control lest news of the affair trigger further sedition. But from this point forward, neither Jugurtha's days or nights provided him any repose; he could hardly trust any place, person, or time; he was afraid of both the enemy and of his own people; he was on guard everywhere and jumped at the sound of any noise; he spent his nights now in one place, now in another, often in circumstances repugnant to the stature of royalty. Sometimes when awakened from sleep he would thrash about in fury and seize hold of his weapons: thus was he tormented by an anxiety that verged on mania.

LXXIII. Now when Metellus heard from deserters about the detection of the anti-Jugurtha plot and of Bomilcar's downfall, he again moved quickly to prepare for another round of war. As Marius continued to pester him about a leave of absence, he finally sent him home, believing that he would be of little use in the field if he were both held against his will and antagonistic towards him. Having dissected the letters that had been sent about Marius and Metellus, the plebians at Rome had accepted with innocent credulity the claims made about both men. Metellus's upper class background, which had previously been a mark of distinction, was now a magnet for animosity; but Marius's humble origins conferred on him the blessing of popular favor. Regardless, partisan feelings rather than each man's good or bad qualities were more determinative of the final outcome.

Subversive magistrates were also inciting the common people; in every political meeting they denounced Metellus while singing the praises of Marius's character. The plebs were finally so

181

whipped up that all the workmen and peasants (whose livelihoods and credit were dependent on their own efforts) abandoned their trades to help Marius, placing their own needs behind his quest for public office. Thus was the nobility hit with a stunning upset: for the first time in many years, the consulship was placed in the hands of a "new man." Later when the people were asked by the tribune Titus Manlius Mancinus whom they wanted as leader when the time came for waging war on Jugurtha, they overwhelmingly demanded Marius. Although shortly before this the senate had assigned Numidia to Metellus, this fact made no difference.

LXXIV. By this time Jugurtha had been deprived of his friends: most he had executed, some had fled in terror to the Romans, and others had escaped to King Bocchus. Since he would be unable to carry on the war without an administrative staff, and he believed it hazardous to take chances on the loyalty of new officers when the old ones had proven to be so back-stabbing, he writhed in perpetual distress. He was satisfied by no situation, no plan, nor any man. He changed his travel itineraries and his commanders day after day; advanced to meet the enemy and at other times retreated into solitude; placed his hopes now in flight and then later in arms; and he did not know which was less trustworthy, his people's bravery or their loyalty. Thus no matter what action he tried to take, he was mired in dilemmas.

While the king was wrestling with these obstacles Metellus suddenly appeared with his army. When the Numidians were prepared and instructed as well as time would permit, the battle was finally joined. In any part of the battle where the king was personally present, the men stood their ground for some time; elsewhere the soldiers were beaten and put to flight after the first engagement. The Romans captured a considerable number of standards and arms, but very few actual combatants; for in nearly all their battles the Numidians look after their feet more than their arms.[221]

LXXV. His hopes dashed by the battle's unfavorable outcome, Jugurtha fled with some fragments of his army and a part of the cavalry to the wild regions of the country. He finally came to Thala, a large and opulent town where his sons were being raised and most of his treasure was stored. After this information found its way to Metellus—and despite the fact that fifty miles of arid and uninhabited wilderness lay between Thala and the closest river—he hoped he could end the war by capturing this town, and so resolved to overcome all obstacles and triumph even over Nature herself. Therefore he ordered that the baggage from every beast of burden should be removed except for ten days' worth of grain rations; to this was added a suitable provision of water to last the same duration. From the surrounding fields he also requisitioned as many domesticated animals as he could find; on these he loaded all types of domestic kit (especially items made of wood) scrounged from the dwellings of the Numidians. In addition he ordered the civilians living in the surrounding area (who had surrendered to Metellus after the king's escape) to bring him as much water as each person could carry; he told them in advance the time and place where they should muster.

From the river that (as we noted above) was the nearest water source to the town, he loaded up the pack animals; and so provisioned, he set out for Thala.[222] Finally when he had come to

---

[221] The wording is: *nam ferme Numidis in omnibus proeliis magis pedes quam arma tuta sunt.* If we assume *pedes* (feet) is meant figuratively, Sallust means the Numidians valued mobility or speed more than weaponry. It is possible, however, that a sly double meaning is intended. Sallust may be saying that the Numidians preferred literally to "safeguard their feet" and flee to save themselves rather than stand and fight.

[222] This town is mentioned in Tacitus (*Ann.* III.21).

the place designated beforehand to the Numidians and his camp had been set up and fortified, it is said that an immense deluge of rain poured down from the sky; so much, in fact, that it was more than sufficient to satisfy his army's entire water needs.[223] In addition the water brought to him was more than he had expected because the Numidians—as is common when a new surrender accord is concluded—had scrupulously honored their agreement. The soldiers preferred to use the rain water, believing it to be a sacred gift; and its appearance did much to boost their morale. For they now believed that they had won the favor of the immortal gods.

Against Jugurtha's expectations, they arrived at Thala the next day. The town's inhabitants, who had believed themselves invulnerable due to the remoteness of their location, were jolted by Metellus's heroic and audacious achievement. But they prepared for action with grim resolution, and our men did the same.

LXXVI. The king now believed that nothing was impossible for Metellus. By the force of his own will he had risen above everything: arms, weapons, terrain, climate, and finally even Nature herself, who directed the destiny of so many others. Jugurtha fled from the town during the night with his children and the majority of his money. After this he never spent more than one day or one night in the same location, pretending that his quick movements were done for the sake of official business. The reality was that he feared betrayal and thought he could avoid it by constant mobility, for treasonous plots require preparation and waiting for favorable opportunities.

---

[223] This was a fortunate event. In the modern era, annual rainfall in northern Tunisia reaches 150 cm (59 in.) annually, while in the south it comes to only 20 cm (8 in.) per year. Data is not of course available for what these numbers were in Metellus's day, but we may presume they were roughly similar.

But when Metellus realized that the townspeople were intent on fighting and that the town was equipped with defensive works and protected by its location, he surrounded the town's walls with a palisaded rampart and a moat.[224] Then in the two most favorable locations he could identify he erected mantlets; he then built a mound, and on top of this set up turret-like fortifications to protect the laborers and their work. In response to this the townspeople rushed to make ready their countermeasures; absolutely nothing was left for either side to do. In the end the Romans—after much labor and exhausted by battles—captured the town forty days after having arrived at its location; but all of the town's loot had been destroyed by the deserters. For when they saw the walls smashed by battering rams and realized their position was hopeless, they brought their gold, silver, and other items they considered precious to the king's residence. There, after indulging in food and wine, they destroyed the treasure, the palace, and themselves in a massive fire. What retribution the defeated had feared from the enemy, they thus willingly administered to themselves.

LXXVII. At the same time that Thala was captured, representatives from the town of Lepcis visited Metellus and asked him to send them a detachment of men along with a commander. They claimed that a certain seditious nobleman named Hamilcar was working behind the scenes for a regime change, and that neither judicial rulings nor the laws were able to keep him in check. They also said that unless Metellus moved quickly, their lives—and the position of their allies—would be in the greatest danger.[225] Now the Lepcitani at the outset of the

---

[224] The military term for this technique is circumvallation.

[225] A vaguely-worded sentence: *ni id festinaret, in summo periculo suam salutem, illorum socios fore.* "Allies" meant the Romans. The idea is that unless Metellus acted decisively, the leadership element of the town would be killed by Hamilcar and the Romans would then lose an ally.

Jugurthine war had petitioned the consul Bestia (and later Rome itself) asking for friendship and a formal alliance. When this request had finally been granted, they had remained loyal and dependable; they had scrupulously carried out all the directives made by Bestia, Albinus, and Metellus. Thus they easily obtained what they sought from the commander.[226] Four cohorts of Ligurians were sent to Lepcis with Caius Annius acting as prefect.

LXXVIII. This town[227] was founded by the Sidonians;[228] we are told that they arrived in this place by boat after fleeing civil chaos at home. It is located between the two Syrtes, a name whose origin is rooted in topographic circumstance. For the Syrtes are two bays near the farthest point of Africa; unequal in size, but equal in character. Near land the bays' waters are quite deep; elsewhere (apparently randomly) it is sometimes deep and sometimes full of shallows. For when the sea swells and begins to rage due to the wind, the waves drag around mud, sand, and large rocks; thus the appearance of each place is changed along with the winds. The name "Syrtes" is derived from this dragging action.[229]

The language of the city has been changed through intermarriage with the Numidians. Its laws and culture are essentially Sidonian; they kept these more easily since they went about their business far from the king's central authority.[230] Between them and the populated areas of Numidia were vast expanses of uninhabited terrain.

LXXIX. Now since we have dealt with the affairs of the people of Lepcis in these regions, it will not be inappropriate to recall an extraordinary and heroic deed of two Carthaginians; the

---

[226] I.e., Metellus gave them what they had asked for.

[227] Lepcis (Leptis Magna).

[228] Sidon, a coastal Phoenician city in what is now Lebanon.

[229] The word Syrtes in Greek is Σύρτις ("shoal") which itself is derived from the verb σύρω, meaning "to drag" or "force away."

[230] I.e., the Numidian king.

place itself reminds us of this incident. During the time when the Carthaginians governed the greater part of Africa, the city of Cyrene was also opulent and powerful. Between the two cities was a sandy expanse of land containing nothing of consequence; there was no river or mountain that might mark the boundary between the two cities. For this reason there was excessive and perpetual war between them.

After the fleets and armies of each city had been routed and scattered, and they had both been worn down to some degree, they agreed to an armistice, fearing that soon some third party might attack them both in their debilitated condition. On a predetermined day envoys were to proceed from each city; at the place where the two parties met would be fixed the common boundary between the two peoples. Two brothers named Philaeni were sent from Carthage; these two moved quickly to complete their transit. The envoys from Cyrene moved more slowly. I do not know whether this was due to laziness or to some legitimate circumstance, but it is normal in these regions to see storms[231] that interfere with travel as much as those on the open ocean. For in these level plateaus that are denuded of vegetation, a gathering wind stirs up sand from the plain, whipping it up with such force that it can be driven into a man's mouth and eyes. Blinded by these conditions, the traveler must delay his journey.

When the envoys from Cyrene realized that they were late and feared punishment back home for the failure of their mission, they accused the Carthaginian envoys of having departed from their city ahead of the agreed time. They abrogated the agreement; indeed they preferred to do anything rather than return home defeated. But when the Carthaginians asked for a new deal—as long as the terms were reasonable—the Greeks made them this proposal: either the Carthaginians could be buried alive at the spot

---

[231] Sand storms.

they wanted as their country's border, or they could let the Cyrene envoys advance as far as they wanted under the same condition. The Philaeni agreed to this arrangement and sacrificed their lives for their country: they were thus buried alive. The Carthaginians dedicated altars[232] to the Philaeni brothers at that location, and decreed other honors for them back at Carthage. I now resume my narrative.

LXXX. After the loss of Thala, Jugurtha thought nothing could stand in Metellus's way. With a few of his men he traveled across vast tracts of wasteland until he came to the region of the Gaetuli, a savage and uncultured race of men who were at that time ignorant of the name of Rome. He gathered a number of them together and taught them in stages to maintain ranks, to follow battle standards, to respond to commands, and to carry out other soldierly tasks. He also won over to his cause the confidants of King Bocchus with considerable bribes and even more generous promises; with their support he was granted access to the king and persuaded Bocchus to launch hostilities against the Romans.

This result was more predictable and easier to accomplish. For at the outset of the war Bocchus had sent envoys to Rome with directions to seek friendship and a security treaty. A few well-placed figures, however, had obstructed this goal (which was so clearly a good idea after the conflict had started) because they could not see beyond their greed. It was normal for them to offer anything for sale, whether honest or dishonest.[233] Before this, one of Jugurtha's daughters had also been married off to Bocchus. But in fact this familial connection counted for very little among the

---

[232] The altars are mentioned by Pliny (*Hist. Nat.* V.4), who presents them as a natural formation of sand. We do not know the extent to which this tale is grounded on fact.

[233] Sallust seems to suggest that Bocchus's envoys were either unable to bribe the right people or had too little money.

Numidians and Moors, as each of them takes as many wives as his finances will allow: sometimes ten, sometimes more, and an even larger number for kings. Thus their attentions are parceled out to an entire group of women. No one woman obtains exclusive status as a man's partner; all of them are considered equally replaceable.[234]

LXXXI. The two armies then came together at an agreed location. There, after assurances were given and received, Jugurtha aroused Bocchu's fighting spirit with his oratory. The oppressive Romans were, he stressed, motivated by an insatiable greed and everyone's common enemy. They had the same pretexts for a war with Bocchus as they had with him and every other nation: a desire to rule over others and an antagonism towards foreign kings. Now it was he who was the target; a little while before it was Carthage and Perses;[235] and in the future the enemy of the Romans would be whoever else appeared to have the most resources. Once he had lectured Bocchus with these and similar pronouncements, the two of them traveled to the town of Cirta, since there Metellus had stashed his plunder, prisoners, and logistical supplies. Thus Jugurtha thought that the capture of the city would prove a decent reward for the trouble; and if the Roman commander arrived on the scene to help his men, he would be able to engage him in open battle. The cunning Numidian knew he must move quickly to deprive his ally Bocchus of any option of enjoying peace with Rome: delays might give rise to doubts and incline the Moorish king to prefer something other than war.[236]

---

[234] *Nulla pro socia optinet, partier omnes viles sunt.* The word *viles* literally means "worthless" or "cheap" but in context this may be too harsh.

[235] King Perses (or Perseus) (c.212—166 B.C.) ruled Macedon from 179 to 168 B.C. The Romans defeated him at the Battle of Pydna in 168 B.C. and after this Macedonia became a Roman province.

[236] By involving Bocchus in the war quickly, Jugurtha wanted to take away

LXXXII. When the commander[237] learned of the partnership of the two kings, he did not rashly plan to engage the enemy in every possible location (as he had often done after defeating Jugurtha). Instead he waited for the kings in a secure camp not far from Cirta. Since a new opponent had entered the war, he believed it was better to gather intelligence on the Moors; this would enhance his preparedness for battle. Meanwhile word had reached him in letters from Rome that Marius had been assigned the province of Numidia; he had learned before this of Marius's election as consul. He was more demoralized by this news than was becoming or honorable, able neither to restrain his tears nor hold his tongue; and although he was an exceptional man as far as other character traits were concerned, he was too willing to indulge his sorrows.[238]

Some believed that his behavior was due to egotism; others thought that an honorable character had been provoked by disrespect; many were convinced that he acted this way because the final victory had been snatched from his hands after he had already won it. For my part, I am convinced that it was more agonizing for him to see Marius honored than it was for him to absorb an insult; he would have experienced much less chagrin if the province taken from him had been handed over to anyone except Marius.

LXXXIII. Thus impeded by his bitter resentment—and believing it was foolish to risk his own neck to fight another man's battles—he sent envoys to King Bocchus with the proposition that should not become an enemy of the Roman people for no good reason. The king had, Metellus stressed, a perfect opportunity that was more useful than war: a chance to form bonds of friendship

---

from him any option of choosing peace over war.

[237] Metellus.

[238] *Nimis molliter aegritudinem pati.* A characteristically Roman sentiment. He "tolerated grief too softly" or was unable to control his pain.

based on mutual interests. Although he might have faith in his own resources, he cautioned, the king should not replace certainty with uncertainty. Without exception, it was easy to start a war but a most difficult task to end one: for its beginning and ending were not within the powers of the same person. Anyone, even an ignorant fool, could launch a war, but it was the victor who would determine its ending.[239] The king should therefore think very carefully about his and his people's interests before entangling his fortunes with Jugurtha's lost cause.

To these points the king responded with words that were disarming enough. He made it clear that he himself eagerly sought peace but had compassion for Jugurtha's plight; everything could be resolved if his Numidian partner were offered an equivalent deal. Metellus again sent messengers to oppose Bocchus's recommendations; the king agreed to some of their counter-offers and rejected others. In this way time dragged on as messengers continually shuttled back and forth; and as Metellus wished, the war remained mired in stalemate.

LXXXIV. Marius, as we have already explained, was elected consul with the enthusiastic backing of the plebian class. After the people assigned the province of Numidia to his responsibility, he began to confront the Roman nobility strenuously and without respite, even though he had been antagonistic to them long before this. Sometimes attacking an individual, at other times attacking them collectively as a class, he harped on the fact that he had snatched the consulship from their defeated hands as a prize of war, and made other statements calculated to aggrandize himself and belittle them. Meanwhile he made it his first priority to take care of the necessary war preparations. He asked for reinforcements for the legions, drafted auxiliaries from friendly

---

[239] The message here is that the victor would not be the same person as the man who started it.

191

nations and kings, and summoned the most daring men from Latium and our allies. Many of these men he was acquainted with from military service while a few he knew only by reputation. Through some vigorous canvassing, he also induced veterans of previous wars to sign up with him.

Although it had adopted an adversarial stance towards Marius, the senate was not prepared to block his activities. It was certainly relieved to order the additional strengthening of the legions, since it thought the plebs were not eager to enlist in the ranks and that Marius would thus lose either his ability to wage war or his popularity with the people. But this expectation turned out to be misplaced: so intense was the fervor for following Marius that had seized the popular mind. Every man dreamed he would return home a victor and be rich with plunder, or nursed other fantasies along these lines. In no small way Marius himself had planted seeds of this sort in their minds with one of his orations. For after everything he had requested from the senate had been passed and he wanted to sign up new soldiers, he convened an assembly of the people in order to encourage prospective soldiers to enroll and—at the same time—to send a message to the nobility. He spoke the following words.

LXXXV. "My fellow Romans, I know that most men do not seek authority from you using the same methods and, after receiving it, use this power in different ways. At first they are hardworking, considerate, and restrained; later they become consumed by laziness and arrogance. But as I see things, the opposite path is the better way. For just as much as the entire republic is worth more than a consulship or praetorship, so much more ought to be the care we take in governing the republic than our concern for chasing after those political positions. I am certainly mindful of this great responsibility I am shouldering at your pleasure.

"To prepare for war while safeguarding the treasury; to draft into military service those whom you do not wish to alienate; to look after all matters foreign and domestic; and to do all this surrounded by jealousy, obstruction, and factionalism is, my fellow Romans, a more difficult task than you might think. Not only this: if another man were to stumble in this job, he could summon help from his old aristocratic family, remind everyone of the notable deeds of his ancestors, or deploy the power of an extended family, clan, and portfolio of clients. All my hopes lie in myself alone and must be safeguarded by my own virtue and integrity. Anything else is unreliable.

"And I well know, my friends, that I am now the focus of everyone's scrutiny. The good and just men support me because my fair-minded policies benefit the republic. The nobility looks for a pretext to attack me. I must work that much harder so that you may not be disenfranchised and that they may be defeated. From the time I was a youth to the present day, I have become used to every kind of labor and personal danger. It is not my intention, my fellow citizens, to stop doing those things I did before my election as consul without any personal benefit now that I have received a reward[240] for doing them. Exercising power judiciously is difficult for those who, due to excessive ambition, pretend to be honest; but as a man who has spent all his years developing the best traits of character, doing the right thing has for me become part of my nature from habit.

"You have instructed me to proceed with the war against Jugurtha, a mandate that the nobility has endured most painfully. I ask you to think very carefully if it would be better to change your minds about this: if you would rather send someone from that gang of nobles to take care of this or some other business, a man from an old family with many portrait masks[241] and no

---

[240] I.e., being elected consul.

[241] Aristocratic Romans were known to keep funeral masks of their ancestors (*imagines maiorum*) in the atrium of a home. These were displayed during

military service. Because he would know nothing he would tremble in fear of everything, bounce mindlessly from one thing to another, and of course enlist someone from the common people to act as an advisor. As a matter of fact, it often happens that the man you choose to command the army looks around for someone to command *him*. My fellow Romans, I have heard of men who have been made consuls who only *after that* begin to read about the deeds of our ancestors and the military treatises of the Greeks. What confused men! Although doing something technically comes after one has first been elected to do something, in the real world actual experience comes first.[242]

"My friends, compare me—a "new man"—with those arrogant nobles. What they are used to hearing or reading, I have either seen first-hand or have done myself. What they have gathered from books I have learned myself while serving as a soldier. Consider now whether you believe actions are worth more than words. They sneer at my common origins, and I at their uselessness. Before me lies my own fate; before them lies their disgrace. I believe there exists one universal nature for all men, and that the bravest has the best pedigree. And if the fathers of Albinus and Bestia could be asked whether they would prefer to have begotten me or them, what do you think their answer would be if they truly wanted the best offspring?

"If by right they look down on me, let them also look down on their own ancestors whose nobility was based, like mine, on masculine virtue. They resent my occupying the office of consul: then let them resent my hard work, my integrity, and the dangers I have risked! For it is through these things that I have achieved

---

funerals. Marius is mocking the type of aristocrat who relies on his name but has no practical military experience.

[242] Meaning that an elected leader should step into the job with a record of real-world experience under his belt.

my office. Men truly corrupted by arrogance live like this; it is as if they think nothing of your honors.[243] But they seek these honors just the same, as if they lived their lives honorably. Delusional are the people who expect that these two completely different things are equal: the delights of idleness and the rewards of virtue. And when they deliver speeches in the senate or to you, they mostly deliver orations praising their ancestors. They think themselves more courageous by recalling these famous exploits. But it is just the opposite. The more distinguished their ancestors' lives are, the more pathetic is their own indolence.

"This surely is the reality: the glory of our ancestors is for future generations something like a bright light, permitting neither good nor bad conduct to remain kept in the dark. I confess my lack of this kind of glory, my fellow citizens. But it is right for me to speak of my own deeds, and this truly is more memorable. See now how unjust these men are! What they arrogate to themselves because of another man's virtue they do not permit me to have as the result of my own. Of course this is because I do not have a collection of ancestor-masks; my nobility is a new one. Certainly it is better to have created a new line than to have dishonored one received as an inheritance.

"Of course I am not unaware that if they want to answer me, there would be a response overflowing with eloquence and rhetorical artifice. But seeing how they slash at us at every chance with vicious words as I serve this public office, it does no good to remain silent, since someone might interpret my restraint as a sign of self-doubt.[244] I am positive that no speech can wound my spirit;

---

[243] By "honors" (*honores*) is meant a prestigious public or political office. Marius is referring to the nobility's contempt for the voting public that decides who will be placed in office.

[244] *Ne quis modestiam in conscientiam duceret.* Sallust's terseness requires us to read between the lines and see that by "conscience" he means "inner doubt as to suitability for office."

if they are forced to use the truth, they have to speak well of me. Lies would directly contradict my life and character.

"But because they find fault in your decision to select me for this office—which is the greatest honor and most important responsibility you have endowed—consider again and again whether you might regret doing this. I cannot point to funeral masks, triumphs, or the consulships of my ancestors to buy your loyalty; but if need be, I can show you spears, flags, insignia and other military trophies, as well as the scars covering my body. These are my "ancestor masks," these my marks of noble rank! They were not given to me as an inheritance as were theirs. I earned them through my own unrelenting labors and experience with danger.

"My words are not put together well, but this is not important to me. Virtue shows itself well enough on its own. It is they who need the rhetorical craftsmanship in order to cover up their repulsive deeds. I have not studied Greek letters, either. I was not inclined to learn them, since they benefitted the virtue of their teachers so little. But I have learned very well the best things for my country: to destroy our enemies, to look after our security, to fear nothing except a shameful reputation, to endure equally the extremes of summer and winter climates, to sleep on the ground, and to suffer toil and deprivation at the same time. I will call on my soldiers to adhere to these same principles. I will not play games with them, promoting myself, making them work hard for the benefit of my personal glory.

"My way is practical; it is in keeping with our civil institutions. To compel your army's obedience with punishments while you yourself are living in softness and luxury is to be a slave-driver, not a true military commander. With these and other methods did your ancestors distinguish themselves and their republic. But the nobility—paying lip service to their ancestors but embracing a very different ethic—look down on us who seek to emulate the great men of the past; they demand that you give them every public office not because of their merit, but because they think you owe them these honors.

"Yet these supremely arrogant men are very much mistaken. Their ancestors left them everything that they could: riches, funeral masks, and their own eternal memory. They did not bequeath them virtue, nor could they. For it alone is neither given nor received as a gift. They say I am vulgar and have uncouth habits because I know little about hosting a fancy banquet, and because I refuse to spend more money at pantomime actors or cooks than I pay my farm manager. This I freely admit, my fellow Romans! For I learned from my father and other distinguished men these things: that delicacy of appearance is appropriate for women, and hard work for men; that all good men should have more glory than riches; and that proficiency with arms, not household furnishings, is what brings distinction.

"What makes them happy, what they believe is worthwhile, let them continue to do. Let them indulge in sex and drink. Let them live out their elder years in the same way they spent their youth: in lavish dinners, ruled by their stomachs and the most indecent parts of the body. Let them leave sweat, dirt, and other such things to us, for whom such things are more pleasing than banquets. But in truth it will not be this way. For when these most repulsive men disgrace themselves with their scandals, they then snatch away the just rewards earned by good people. What is most unfair is that their extravagance and laziness—the most despicable of habits—never seem to hurt those who indulge in them, yet turn out to be the ruin of our blameless republic.[245]

"Now that I have answered them with words sufficient to satisfy my honor (yet insufficient to compare with their depravity), I will say a few words about our republic. First of all,

---

[245] Readers will not fail to miss the contemporary resonance and import of these words.

have confidence about the situation in Numidia, my friends. For you have now removed all the things that were protecting Jugurtha until the present time: greed, ineptitude, and arrogance. There is now an army in Numidia that knows the country. But by Hercules![246] It is more tenacious than lucky. A large part of it has been frittered away through the greed and bad judgment of its commanders. So I say to you men of military age: join me and take charge of your republic. No man should feel fear because of the terrible blunders of others or the egotism of generals.

"I, your captain, will be with you on the march and in battle, and the comrade of your danger as well. I will lead you and myself as one unit in every way. And surely with the help of the immortal gods everything is about ready to happen: victory, plunder, glory. Even if these things were in doubt or a long way off, every good man should still rally to the aid of the republic. In fact no one ever became immortal through faintheartedness. No parent ever wanted his child to live forever: he would rather his son live life as a good and honest man. I would say more, fellow Romans, if words could grant virtue to the timid. For the brave I think the words I have spoken are enough."

LXXXVI. When Marius saw that he had aroused the minds of the people after delivering his speech in this way, he immediately outfitted his transport ships with supplies, payrolls, arms, and other logistical necessities. He also ordered his deputy Aulus Manlius to depart with these cargoes. He himself meanwhile enlisted soldiers not according to social class in the manner of our ancestors, but rather opening the rolls to anyone who wished to sign up. Most of these volunteers came from the "head count" category.[247] Some commenters believe he did this from a lack of

---

[246] An interjection (*mehercule*) similar to "My God!"

[247] This was a major development in enlistment practices. The term used for "head count" is *capite censi* (literally "those counted by the head"). Rome's

198

suitable draftees; others say he was simply trying to gain favor with the common people as their consul, since he had been elevated and favored by this class. He who is most desperate is the most useful for an ambitious man seeking power; because he has nothing, he is not worried about preserving wealth. For him, anything that brings him a salary is considered respectable.

Marius thus set out for Africa with many more men than he had officially been allotted. A few days later he landed at Utica; there the command of the army was delivered to him by the executive officer Publius Rutilius. For Metellus had sidestepped an encounter with Marius, lest he have to witness what his spirit had been unable even to endure hearing.

LXXXVII. When the consul had filled the legions and cohorts with auxiliaries, he set out for fertile districts laden with potential spoils; he gave all seized goods to his soldiers, then attacked nearby fortresses and towns insufficiently protected by geography or men. He made contact with the enemy in various locations and fought numerous minor engagements. Meanwhile the new soldiers entered battle without fear. They saw that those who fled were either captured or killed; the bravest were the safest. They began to realize that what safeguarded liberty, country, parents, and everything else—and what secured glory and riches—was arms. Within a short time the recruits and veterans were fused together as one, and so was the martial virtue of all made equal.

---

original military enlistment system was based on wealth and property ownership. Only those who had appreciable wealth could enlist in the legions. According to Livy (I.43) there were five identifiable classes from highest to lowest measured by *asses* (the Roman unit of currency). Those who owned no significant property (i.e., the poorest Romans) were "counted by the head" rather than evaluated by what they owned. They were exempt from military service. By allowing anyone to sign up—and inevitably making such enlistees dependent on him personally—Marius was establishing a precedent that years later would eventually undermine the senate's authority.

But when the kings[248] became aware of Marius's arrival, they each retreated to separate impervious locations. This development pleased Jugurtha, who hoped a divided enemy would be more vulnerable to attack;[249] he also thought that the Romans, like many others, would be more lax and unrestrained in conduct when freed from fear.

LXXXVIII. When Metellus meanwhile arrived back at Rome he was received—to his surprise—with a great outpouring of public enthusiasm. The ill-feeling against him had evaporated, and he basked in the favor of plebians and patricians alike. Marius energetically and sensibly attended both to his own men and the threat from the enemy; he learned what things were good or bad for both sides, reconnoitered the movements of the two kings and predicted their schemes and stratagems, always maintaining the highest operational intensity and permitting the enemy no respite. He often attacked the Gaetulians and Jugurtha while they were seizing plunder from our allies. They were put to flight; and the king himself was deprived of his arms not far from the town of Cirta. But when he saw that these engagements, though bringing him some temporary glory, did not force the war to a conclusion, he resolved to surround every city that was most useful to the enemy (either because of the armed men stationed there or because of its location) and most opposed to his own objectives.[250] Jugurtha, he hoped, would either be stripped of his field units if he accepted this situation, or would be forced to commit himself in open battle.

---

[248] Jugurtha and Bocchus.

[249] I.e., he hoped Marius would divide his own forces to pursue Bocchus and himself separately.

[250] He proposed to surround (*circumvenire*) the population centers to deprive the insurgents of local support and supplies. This is a classic counterinsurgency tactic, used with some success by the British during later phases of the Boer War of 1899-1902.

Bocchus, for his part, regularly dispatched messengers to Marius. He claimed to desire the friendship of the Roman people and assured the commander that he need fear no hostile move from him. Whether this was a ruse, so calculated that an unexpected blow would hit Marius with greater force, or whether Bocchus's unstable temperament caused him to swing wildly between aggression and passivity, has never been adequately explained.

LXXXIX. In accordance with his strategy, the consul targeted the fortified towns and strongpoints, sometimes using force and at other times deploying bribery or intimidation, and succeeded in making them switch sides. Initially his efforts were rather mild, as he believed Jugurtha would make the protection of his people a matter of personal attention. But when he realized that the king was far removed from the scene and absorbed in other issues, he knew that the time had come to attack with more frequent and greater intensity.

There was a large and strong town named Capsa situated in a wide tract of uninhabited land; in local tradition its founder is named as the Libyan Hercules. Under Jugurtha's regime its people were exempt from taxation and governed mildly; for this reason its people were considered his most loyal subjects. The town was fortified against potential enemies not only by walls, defensive weapons, and men, but also by the severity of the terrain where it was located. Outside Cirta's immediate vicinity the entire region was barren, uncultivated, completely parched, and teeming with snakes;[251] like all wild animals, their aggressiveness was made even more pronounced by the terrain's insufficient food. Besides this reality about snakes, we should note that the toxicity of snake venom itself is increased more by the animal's thirst than other factors.

---

[251] Cirta's location can be seen in the map section at the beginning of the *War of Jugurtha*.

The capture of this town became an object of supreme desire for Marius. Besides its military significance, it also seemed a considerable challenge; and Metellus (he remembered) had secured glory for himself by the storming of Thala. The two towns were not much different in topographic conditions and defensive fortifications, except that at Thala there were several fresh water springs not far from the city walls. The inhabitants of Capsa had only one water source, a flowing spring located within the city; rainwater provided the only other option. Because the Numidians mostly lived on milk and the flesh of wild game, and sought out neither salt nor other stimuli for the palate, this kind of situation was willingly tolerated in Africa for those living an unsophisticated life a great distance inland. For them food was a tool to ward off hunger and thirst rather than an intoxicant to slake one's lust or extravagance.[252]

XC. So the consul, after weighing all his options, simply put his faith in the gods; for his own plans were inadequate to address the difficulties presented by the situation. Indeed he was even faced with a shortage of available grain. The Numidians care more about using arable land for grazing than for tillage, and any grain that had been available was already brought to secure locations by the king's orders. In addition, since it was the end of the summer season, the fields at this time were dry and unfit for agricultural use. Nevertheless he was still able to provide his army with sufficient resources. He turned over to the auxiliary cavalry all the cattle that had been captured in the preceding days, and ordered his deputy Aulus Manlius to go with the lightly-armed cohorts to the town of Laris, where the payrolls and logistical supplies were

---

[252] Sallust is not so much here describing Numidians as he is condemning Romans. The historian Tacitus would later use the same device when he praised the supposedly virtuous simplicity of the barbarian Germans in his *De origine et situ Germanorum*.

located. Marius said he himself would come there after a few more days spent plundering what he needed in the area. Thus concealing his true designs, he set out for the river Tana.[253]

XCI. Every day during the march Marius distributed the cattle uniformly among the centuries and the cavalry squadrons, directing that waterskins be fashioned from the animal hides. This alleviated their lack of grain and prepared, without anyone being aware, something that would soon prove to be of great advantage. When they finally came to the river on the sixth day of the march, a great quantity of skins had been made. There he constructed a lightly-armed camp, ordering his men to eat a meal and be ready to move out at nightfall. Discarding all their belongings, they loaded the pack-mules and themselves with water only. When Marius decided the time was right, he set out from the camp, marched all through the night, and then stopped. The next day was the same; finally on the third day long before sunrise he arrived at an area of undulating terrain that was not more than two miles distant from Capsa. There Marius paused with his entire force, trying to avoid detection as best he could.

When the new day came and many Numidians—totally oblivious to the possibility of attack—began to go out from the town, he at once ordered all the cavalry and with them the fastest infantrymen to make a direct charge on Capsa and attack the city gates. Marius himself followed soon after, carefully watching his units and not permitting them to pillage. By the time the Capsans realized the full dimensions of what was happening, their confusion, their mounting terror, their crippling shock at the

---

[253] The Latin text gives the spelling of the river's name as Tanaïs. The river was apparently located between Laris and Capsa. Laris (or Lares) was a town in western Numidia to the south of Cirta; its modern name in Tunisia is Henchir Lorbeus. *See* Crooks, G.R. & Schem, A.J., *A Latin-English School Lexicon*, Philadelphia: J.B. Lippincott & Co., 1861.

unforeseen disaster, and their knowledge that a good part of their people were trapped outside the city walls at the mercy of the enemy, finally obliged them to surrender. But the town was burned to the ground; the adult Numidian males were put to death and all the rest sold into slavery; and the soldiers divided up the spoils.[254] This action contravened the rules of war, but it was not based on malice or greed. It had been a critical base for Jugurtha and was difficult for us to reach; its people were capricious, unreliable, and had already proven to be uncontrollable by either magnanimity or fear.

XCII. He had always been regarded as a great and illustrious man; but after Marius carried through this victory without any significant detriment to his men, he began to be seen as even greater and more awe-inspiring. All his ill-considered moves were seen as coming from a position of virtue. The soldiers serving under his lenient hand—and enriched by him—lauded him to the heavens; the Numidians feared him as if he were superhuman. In the end everyone—friend and foe alike—believed he exercised mystical powers or that he could foretell events through some divine will.

But the consul set out for other towns after things had gone well for him at Capsa. He seized a few after some defensive fighting by the Numidians; but most of the towns, aware of the horrific fate of the Capsans, had been deserted and set on fire. Sorrow and carnage were present everywhere. Finally, after occupying much territory with mostly bloodless victories for his army, he undertook another operation, not as perilous as that against Capsa, yet equally challenging.

---

[254] The poetic beauty of this typically Sallustian sentence almost mitigates the terrible reality it describes. I cannot resist quoting it: *Ceterum oppidum incensum, Numidae puberes interfecti, alii omnes venumdati, praeda militibus divisa.*

Not far from the Muluccha River[255] (which separated the kingdoms of Jugurtha and Bocchus) there was in the middle of a plateau a rocky elevation expansive enough to accommodate a medium-sized fortress. It was accessible by one narrow trail; the entire terrain feature was naturally steep as if it had been so fashioned by engineering and careful planning. Because the king's treasures were stored here, this was the objective that Marius intended to seize with the utmost resolution. But this exploit was carried out more with the intervention of luck than by means of careful planning. For the fortress was bristling with arms and men, and had sufficient grain supplies as well as a water spring. The location was unsuitable for using ramparts, towers, and other types of siege devices; and the path to the citadel was extremely narrow with cliffs on either side. Mantlets were employed with great danger to the men but to no avail; for they were destroyed by fire or stones as soon as they moved forward just a little bit. Because of the uneven ground the soldiers could neither take up secure positions nor operate inside the mantlets without danger: the best men were slain or injured, and fear overwhelmed the rest.

XCIII. After devoting many days to these labors, a troubled Marius wondered whether he should give up the entire operation as hopeless or await the intervention of fortune, which had often been useful to him in the past. For many days and nights he fretted and seethed; then by chance a Ligurian, a rank-and-file soldier of the auxiliary cohorts, while leaving camp to collect water not far from the side of the fortress that was farthest from the fighting, noticed snails crawling among the rocks. Collecting one after the other, and then even more, his dedication to harvesting the

---

[255] This river is also mentioned in chapters XIX and CX. It was located about five hundred miles west of Cirta.

animals brought him little by little almost to the mountain's summit. After reflecting on his solitude there, a desire to accomplish a supremely difficult task—which is a trait of the human race—began to burn within him.

By chance in this place a great oak tree[256] had grown among the rocks; the lower part of its trunk was in a direction parallel to the ground, but then it curved and stretched upward, as all growing things do by nature. Making use of the branches of this tree and the surrounding rocks, the Ligurian reached the plateau of the stronghold at a time when all the Numidians had their attentions fixed on the fighting that was taking place. After studying all that he thought would be useful later, he went back down the mountain the same way: not blindly as he had ascended, but probing and inspecting everything. He then went directly to Marius and told him what he had learned, pleading with him to attack the fortress at the place where he himself had scaled the mountain. He volunteered to lead another ascent and direct this dangerous mission.

Marius sent some men to go with the Ligurian and learn more about his scheme; each observer claimed it would be difficult or easy according to his own personal character. Nevertheless, the consul's first impressions were generally positive. He thus selected five of the most physically fit trumpeters and hornblowers[257] present, along with four centurions to go with them as security; all of these men were told to obey the Ligurian. The following day was scheduled for the start of the operation.

XCIV. When he saw that the time had come to move out, he made the final preparations, collected the requisite items, and brought his team to the ascension point. Those who would be

---

[256] Sallust identifies this tree as an *ilex*, which can mean the holm-oak or the kermes oak. *See* Pliny, *Hist. Nat.* XVI.19 and XVI.32

[257] The *tubicen* (tuba) and *cornicen* (trumpet) were used by Roman military units to convey orders, signals, or messages in the field.

scaling the mountain changed their weapons and gear as instructed by the Ligurian. Their feet and heads were bare so that their uphill vision and movement would be easier in the midst of the mountain's rock projections; swords and shields were slung on their backs, and they carried Numidian shields made from layered animal skins on account of their lighter weight and because they made less noise when jostled. The Ligurian then started the ascent, tying ropes to suitable rocks and old roots to help the other soldiers climb more easily. Sometimes he personally assisted those comrades who were apprehensive about the difficulty of the ascent; and where the route was especially difficult, he sent the men ahead of him unarmed one after the other and would then follow behind with their weapons. It was he who took the lead in testing the hazardous points in the route; and by often clambering up and coming down at such places (and then getting out of the way), he built up the confidence of the other climbers.

Thus after a long time and a tremendous effort they arrived at the citadel in a part of it that was unmanned, since all the defenders were then oriented—just as on other days—in the direction of the enemy.[258] When Marius learned from messengers that the Ligurian had reached his objective, he urged his men

---

[258] It is surprising that the Numidians had no sentries or watches posted on the other side of the fortress, but such complacency is not uncommon in the annals of war. "Impregnable" fortifications promote a sense of invulnerability that determined attackers can exploit. Fixed strongpoints have been shown time and time again to be much weaker than their defenders believe. Consider the Roman general Belisarius's capture of Naples during the Gothic War (A.D. 535—554) as told in Procopius's *History of the Wars* (V.8); the German Army's daring seizure of the Belgian fortress of Eben Emael in 1940; or the British attack on Quebec in 1759 during the Seven Years' War. It was not without reason that Machiavelli, in his *Discourses* (II.24), judged fixed fortifications to be more harmful than useful.

forward with renewed intensity; he himself left the safety of the mantlets, set up a *testudo*,[259] and pushed forward. At the same time he terrorized the enemy from a distance using missiles, arrows, and slingers. But since the Numidians had often previously knocked over and burned the Romans' mantlets, they were not in the habit of seeking cover within the fortress's walls; they moved around outside the walls both day and night, shouting obscenities at the Romans and nearly causing Marius to lose his composure. They even taunted our soldiers by saying that Jugurtha would enslave them: so arrogant had they become by their repeated successes.

While all this was happening—with the Romans and their enemies absorbed in battle, each side fighting to the limit of its endurance, one for glory and power and the other for security— suddenly there erupted from the far side of the fortress the sound of a battle-call.[260] At first the women and children, who were present as spectators to the fighting, turned and fled; then those who were closest to the wall did the same; and finally every person armed or unarmed took to flight. Once this occurred the Romans pursued them more intensely, scattering but only wounding most. Hungry for glory and struggling to reach the walls, the soldiers clambered over the bodies of the fallen. Not one man paused to search for plunder. Thus redeemed by fortune did Marius's temerity manage to snatch glory from the jaws of culpability.[261]

---

[259] The *testudo* ("tortoise shell") was an infantry combat technique where a unit encased itself in protective "armor" by overlapping raised shields above the heads of the men and on the four sides of the formation.

[260] A *signum*, the sound given off by a *tubicen* or *cornicen*.

[261] Meaning that his gamble in using the Ligurian's ruse had paid off and saved Marius from defeat (and blame back in Rome). Sallust's austere words are *sic forte correcta Mari temeritas gloriam ex culpa invenit*.

XCV. In the midst of these events, the quaestor Lucius Sulla[262] arrived in camp with a large cavalry force that he had raised from Latium (and other allies) and had been garrisoned at Rome. Because the appearance of Sulla's name reminds us of this great man's importance to history, it is appropriate for us to state some facts regarding his character and personal qualities. In no other place will we discuss Sulla's career. Lucius Sisenna, who described him more fully and diligently than any other historian writing on the subject, has censored his own words a little too much, I believe.[263]

Sulla was a nobleman of old patrician stock, but the family line had nearly come to an end due to the indolence of his ancestors. He was learned in both Greek and Latin letters, a man of expansive intelligence, fond of pleasures of the flesh but a lover of glory even more. He maintained himself in luxurious leisure, yet his sensual pursuits never kept him from affairs of state. As a married man, however, he might have treated his wife with a bit more respect. Eloquent, cunning, and able to form friendships with ease, he possessed an unrivalled innate capability for camouflaging his true intentions, yet he was greathearted in many things, especially with money. He was the most fortunate[264] of all

---

[262] Lucius Cornelius Sulla (138 B.C.—78 B.C.) would later go on to become dictator in 82 or 81 B.C. He retired from office near the end of 81 B.C. but his proscriptions of opponents and overall ruthlessness would set destabilizing precedents.

[263] Lucius Cornelius Sisenna (c. 120 B.C.—67 B.C.) was a soldier and historian who wrote a history of his times in twenty-three books, none of which have survived. *See* Velleius Paterculis II.9. If he downplayed the unpleasant realities of Sulla's career, it is either because he feared being added to one of Sulla's proscription lists or because he was one of his partisans.

[264] Sulla's nickname was *Felix* ("the happy" or "the fortunate").

men before his triumph in the civil war;[265] but in his case fortune never was a substitute for hard work, although many have questioned which was more decisive, his vigor or his luck. With regard to the things he did later, I am uncertain whether one should more feel shame or chagrin to recount them.[266]

XCVI. As we noted above, after Sulla arrived with his cavalry in Marius's camp in Africa, he quickly became the most capable man there despite having no prior military training or experience. He addressed the men with respect, providing favors to many when they asked and to others at his own pleasure; yet was reluctant to accept favors himself and repaid them more quickly than borrowed money. He himself never tried to collect a debt, but preferred instead to have as many men as possible owe him something. He could joke or speak seriously with the commonest of men and joined them while they worked, during marches, or at sentry duty; at the same time he did not, like some schemer inclined to mischief, undermine the consul's reputation or that of any other good man. His only focus was to allow no one to outshine him in military planning or performance; and in this he was ahead of the vast majority. By displaying these traits and habits, Sulla quickly endeared himself both to Marius and the men.

XCVII. After having lost the town of Capsa and various fortified positions that were useful to him (as well as a great deal of money), Jugurtha sent messengers to Bocchus, imploring him

---

[265] Sulla waged several wars against political opponents (Caius Marius and Lucius Cornelius Cinna) from 88 B.C. to 80 B.C. before emerging as dictator.
[266] Referring to Sulla's purges of his opponents (real and suspected) after his victory. A very Sallustian sentence: *Nam postea quae fecerit, incertum habeo pudeat an pigeat magis disserere.* I prefer to translate *pigeat* as "chagrin" rather than "disgust" since the former word preserves the alliteration in the original.

to move his forces into Numidia; he was convinced that the time for a decisive battle had come.[267] But when he learned Bocchus was balking at the idea and still pondering the rationales for peace and war, he sent bribes again to the king's associates as before and promised to give the Moor one-third of Numidia's territory if the Romans were expelled from Africa or if the war were concluded with his original borders intact. Enticed by this promise, Bocchus came over to Jugurtha's side with a great number of men. Once their two armies were joined together, they went on the offensive against Marius as he was moving to garrison his troops for the winter; the attack came at a time when only a tenth part of the day remained.[268] They thought that the darkness—which was coming soon—would shield them if they were beaten yet be no impediment if they defeated the Romans, since they knew the terrain well. For the Romans, on the other hand, darkness would be more difficult in either case.

But as soon as the consul was made aware from his various sources that the enemy was coming, the opposing army itself actually appeared. And before the Roman ranks could be properly arranged or the baggage train organized—even before any signal or command could be issued—the Moorish and Gaetulian cavalry smashed into Marius's army, not in organized formation or according to any battle tactics, but purely *en masse*, just as if chance had rolled them into one ball of fury. Although shocked by this terror coming from nowhere, the soldiers were nevertheless mindful of their martial virtue: they either took up arms or protected others who were trying to prepare their gear for combat. Some mounted horses and attacked the enemy directly. The fight more resembled a melee between criminal gangs than a

---

[267] Because if he waited longer his fighting capacity would be degraded beyond the point of recovery.

[268] I.e., close to dusk.

formal, set-piece battle; without standards and without set ranks, infantry and cavalry were hurled together in chaos, with some units falling back and others being cut down; many who were fighting ferociously against the enemy were enveloped from behind. Since the enemy had a superiority in numbers and inundated the Romans on every side, neither martial virtue nor arms were enough to protect a man. Finally the Roman recruits and seasoned veterans—the latter being experienced in war— formed a ring (as chance or their location brought them together) and so immediately shielded themselves from every direction and, so organized, held out against the enemy's attacks.

XCVIII. In this terrible hour Marius was neither paralyzed by fear nor more demoralized than before. With his cavalry squadron, which was composed of his best fighters rather than his closest friends, he rushed from place to place to help the men who were in dire need, even attacking the enemy where they opposed him with the largest troop concentrations. Because it was impossible to issue standard verbal orders due to the chaos and din of combat, he issued his orders by hand signals. Eventually daylight expired; yet the barbarians did not relent in any way. They pressed the Romans even more intensely, believing—as their kings had promised them—that the onset of night would be to their advantage.

Deriving his next move from the disposition of forces on the ground and needing a location where his men could retreat, Marius occupied two hills that were close together. One of these hills was not large enough to accommodate a camp but had a large spring of water; the other hill was suitable for his purpose because it was generally steep and elevated, thus needing little fortification. He ordered Sulla to position himself by the spring during the night with the cavalry. Marius himself gradually pieced together his dispersed soldiers—no less disoriented from all the enemy attacks—and fast-marched[269] them to the hill. Thus the two kings, compelled by the difficulties presented by Marius's position, were deterred from continuing the battle.

Nevertheless they did not permit their men to go too far away; setting up scattered camps, they surrounded both hills with a huge number of men. Finally after building a sea of bonfires the barbarians, as is their custom, spent most of the night in celebration. They were ecstatic, shouting at the top of their lungs; even their arrogant leaders acted as if they had already won simply because they had not fled the battlefield. But from their elevated position in the darkness, the Romans could see all of this quite clearly, and it greatly aided their resolution.

XCIX. Marius was very much reassured by the enemy's inexperience in the ways of war. He gave strict instructions that his men should keep as quiet as possible, not even to "sound off" when it was time to replace the night watches. Then as daylight approached—and with the enemy worn out and overtaken by sleep—he suddenly ordered the men standing watch and the horn-blowers of the legions, squadrons, and cohorts to blast out a signal all at once, and for the soldiers to scream war-cries as they burst out of the camp's gates. The Moors and Gaetulians, suddenly awakened and confused by the terrible noises, were unable to flee, take up arms, help each other, or do anything at all. Amid the roar of battle, the shouting, the feeling of helplessness, the disorder, the panic, and the sheer velocity of the Roman attack, something like madness gripped them all. In the end they were crushed and routed. Most of their military standards and weapons were captured; more of the enemy was slain in this battle than in all others that had preceded it. For their escape had been hindered by sleep and by the terror that came without warning.

---

[269] The phrase used is *pleno gradu*, literally meaning "at a full step." "Double-time march" would also convey the intended meaning.

C. Marius finally moved to his winter quarters as he had previously intended to do; he opted to settle in the maritime towns due to their convenient supply lines.[270] He became neither sluggish nor conceited on account of his victory and proceeded in a defensive order of battle[271] under the watchful eyes of the enemy. Sulla was positioned with his cavalry on Marius's right; on the left flank Aulus Manlius kept watch with the slingers, bowmen, and Ligurian cohorts. The tribunes with the maniples of lightly-armed men were located in the front and rear. The deserters, whose lives were worth the least but who possessed unrivaled knowledge of the area, conducted reconnaissance on the enemy's avenues of movement. At the same time the consul responded to everything as if he had no rigid operating procedures in place; he was present everywhere, praising or rebuking the men as the situation dictated. He himself was armed and watchful in every way, and demanded the same from his men.

With the same attention to detail that he showed on the march, he built his camp, assigned cohorts from the legions to guard the gate, and sent the auxiliary cavalry to watch the front of the camp. He placed other men on top of the ramparts in the defensive bulwarks. He himself made contact with the guards on watch, not because he lacked confidence that they would perform as ordered, but rather so that the individual initiative of the soldiers would be equal to exertion of their commander. At this and other times during the Jugurthine war, Marius sensibly governed his army

---

[270] I.e., the towns along the Mediterranean coast could easily receive provisions from Italy.

[271] The "square formation" (*quadrato agmine*) is a defensive order of battle mentioned in Livy (II.6.6: *Valerius quadrato agmine peditem ducit...*). It is also described in Quintus Curtius's *Historiae* (V.1.19 and V.13.10) and in Ammianus Marcellinus (XXIX.5.39). The idea was that the army would form a square to protect itself in hostile territory, with the logistical supplies placed within the square.

more by appealing to its sense of duty than through corporal punishment. Many said this was because of his need to feel popular, and that from his early years he was accustomed to see hardship—and other things that most people would call miserable—as enjoyable. Whatever the reason, our republic benefitted as much and as gloriously as if he had used the severest physical methods of control.

CI. On the fourth day, not far from the town of Cirta, Marius's reconnaissance elements appeared at once from every direction in haste; this was an indication that the enemy was near. But since the various returning scouts all provided the same information despite coming from different directions, the consul was uncertain as to what type of battle formation to employ. He therefore remained in place, kept his current battle order unchanged,[272] and prepared for anything that might happen. This dashed the hopes of Jugurtha, who had divided his forces into four parts, believing that if they maneuvered against Marius's four sides at the same time, at least some of them would strike the Romans from behind.

Meanwhile Sulla—with whom the enemy had made contact first—rallied his men and attacked the Moors with some of his men using cavalry squadrons one after the other formed as tightly as possible. The rest of his force stayed in place, protecting their bodies from the projectile weapons thrown at them from a distance; those who came within arms' reach of the Romans were cut down. While the cavalry forces were in this way locked in battle, Bocchus with his infantry (commanded by his son Volux) assaulted the back of the Roman formation. This infantry had not been at the previous fight due to delays on the march. Marius at that time was at the front, since Jugurtha was there with most of his men. But once he learned of Bocchus's arrival on the scene,

---

[272] I.e., the square formation used on the march.

Jugurtha with a few men secretly repositioned himself with this new infantry force.[273] He then shouted out in Latin (for he had learned to speak it at Numantia) that our men fought to no avail because he had killed Marius with his own hand a short time before. At the same time he waved a sword darkened with gore that had been bloodied during the battle by the efficient killing of one of our infantrymen. When the soldiers heard this statement, they were shocked more by the idea of such an atrocity than by any belief that it was true; at the same time the barbarians' spirits were raised and they proceeded to attack the unnerved Romans that much more intensely.

Marius's men were close to defeat when Sulla, having beaten the enemies he was facing, came back and assaulted the flank of the Moorish force. Bocchus collapsed at once. But Jugurtha, despite wanting to prop up his men and hold on to the victory that was in his hands, was surrounded by cavalrymen; and while everyone to his left and right was killed, he slipped away alone with hostile weapons everywhere around him. In the meantime Marius, having routed the cavalry, rushed to help his men whom he had heard were stretched to the point of collapse. The enemy was finally driven off everywhere. Then on the open fields a horrific scene came into view: chasing, fleeing, slaughtering, capturing, and horses and men strewn everywhere. Many of the wounded were unable either to get away or to suffer in silence; some tried to stand and immediately fell over again. As far as one's vision extended were weapons, arms, and dead bodies mingling with the blood-soaked earth that embraced them all.

CII. Without doubt now the undisputed victor, the consul moved from this place to the town of Cirta, which had been his objective from the beginning. Five days after the barbarians had

---

[273] Meaning that Jugurtha slipped away from the front and moved to the rear to be with Bocchus's infantry.

been bested a second time on the battlefield, envoys from Bocchus came to the town, asking Marius on behalf of the king that he send him two of his most trusted deputies. Bocchus wanted to discuss, they said, matters of common concern between himself and the Roman people. The consul at once ordered Lucius Sulla and Aulus Manlius to go. Although they were going under a summons request, it still seemed advisable to say a few words of their own to the king. They might change his mind if he was inclined against them, or make him more eager for peace if he was already predisposed to it. Therefore Sulla—to whom Manlius yielded not because of his seniority but because of his greater eloquence— made a few remarks to the following effect:

"King Bocchus, it brings us great happiness to know that the gods have finally counseled you, so great a man, to select the path of peace rather than that of war; that you, the best of men, choose no longer to associate with Jugurtha, who represents the worst; and at the same time to relieve us of the bitter obligation of equating your reasonable error with his abominable crimes. In this regard I note that the Roman people, from the inception of their rule, have thought it better to seek friends rather than slaves; it was safer, they believed, to govern by consent rather than force. Our friendship is truly most ideal for you: first, because we are a long way off, thus less a chance for trouble between us but giving you the same benefit as if were close by; secondly, because we already have enough people to look after, whereas neither we nor anyone else ever had enough allies. I only wish that you had thought this way from the beginning! Certainly by this time you would have received many more benefits from the Roman people than the negative experiences you have endured.

"But since fortune usually rules the affairs of men, it appears to be her desire that you should taste both our military power and our goodwill. And because this is what she sees as right, move forward to do what you set out to do. You have many opportunities easily to replace your mistakes with correct duties.

Let this sentiment make its way to your heart: never have the Roman people been equaled in the art of showing goodwill. For you already know what it can do when it comes to war."

To these remarks Bocchus responded calmly and politely, at the same time offering a few words about why he had acted as he did. He had taken up arms, he maintained, not out of a spirit of aggression but to protect his kingdom. He had expelled Jugurtha from a part of Numidia that had become his by the law of war; he could not, he said, then tolerate Marius's plundering of this same land. In addition, when he had previously sent envoys to Rome asking for a treaty of friendship, his initiative had been rebuffed. But he said he was willing to let the past go; and if Marius allowed it, he would dispatch envoys again to the senate. Yet once this request was allowed, the barbarian's mind was changed by his friends. Jugurtha, fearing the outcome of a peace conference upon learning of the diplomatic shuttle of Sulla and Manlius, had bribed Bocchus's associates.

CIII. Once Marius had established his forces in their winter encampments, he headed to a thinly populated area with the lightly-armed cohorts and some cavalry in order to attack one of the king's fortresses; Jugurtha had manned this citadel exclusively with deserters. Either because his memories of what had happened to him in two previous battles returned (or because of the admonitions he had been given by friends whom Jugurtha was unable to bribe), Bocchus once again chose, out of all his confidants, five relatives of known integrity and superlative ability. He ordered these five to go to Marius and, if the situation called for it, to Rome; he permitted them considerable leeway in the conduct of negotiations as well as authorization to conclude the war on whatever terms necessary. These men left early for the Roman winter camp. While en route, however, they were waylaid and robbed by Gaetulian bandits; they then fled in fear and humiliation to Sulla, whom the consul had left in charge after setting out on his mission.[274] Sulla did not see them as enemies or as suspicious, as the circumstances might have merited, but received them with consideration and courtesy. From this incident the barbarians concluded that the Romans' reputation for greed was unjustified and that Sulla, because of his magnanimity towards them, could become a friend.

For many of them were unacquainted with the concept of generosity; anyone who extended generosity was thought to be favorably disposed to the other party. All gifts were considered proof of sincere goodwill. They therefore disclosed to the quaestor what Bocchus had ordered them to do. At the same time they pleaded with him to assist them with his influence and counsel. With fine words they extolled the king's riches, reputation, greatness and other qualities that they believed would give them leverage or good favor. After Sulla finally made them all the requisite promises and gave them guidance on how to deal with Marius and speak to the Roman senate, the envoys lingered there with him for about forty days.

CIV. Marius returned to Cirta after taking care of the business he had planned to do. When he learned of the arrival of the envoys, he ordered them and Sulla to come from Utica; so ordered also from Utica were the praetor Lucius Bellienus and all members of the senatorial class in the region. In this way he learned the specifics of Bocchus's offers. The envoys' ability to go to Rome came under consideration; in the meantime an armistice was requested from the consul. This pleased Sulla and the rest of the delegates present; a few were determined to maintain a hostile posture, no doubt ignorant of the fact that human affairs—always in flux and unreliable—are always changing to favor one side or another.

Once the Moors had procured everything they wanted, three

---

[274] I.e., the expedition to attack one of Jugurtha's fortresses in the desert.

of them left for Rome with Gnaeus Octavius Ruso, the quaestor who had transported the soldiers' payrolls to Africa. Two of them returned to Bocchus. The king listened to what they had to say with great relief, especially the details about Sulla's generosity and consideration. After asking for pardon by claiming their king had erred and been manipulated by Jugurtha's criminal intentions, they requested a formal treaty of friendship. This was the response: "The senate and the Roman people are in the habit of remembering both kindnesses and injuries. But because Bocchus expresses remorse for his actions, Rome forgives him for this offense. When he shows himself worthy, friendship and a formal treaty will be granted."[275]

CV. On learning of these developments, Bocchus asked Marius through a letter if he could send Sulla to him, so that the two of them[276] could discuss matters of common concern. Marius sent Sulla with a detachment of cavalry and Balearic slingers.[277] Traveling with him also were archers and a cohort of Paelignians;[278] they were lightly armed due to the need for speed. Since the enemy's spears were light, this type of armor afforded sufficient protection. But on the fifth day of the journey Bocchus's son Volux, suddenly showed himself on open terrain along with not more than a thousand cavalrymen; but since they were moving around in agitation and disorder, their number seemed to Sulla and everyone else to be much greater than it was. This generated anxiety about the enemy's intentions. Each man thus made

---

[275] Meaning, of course, that he must prove himself by some act in Rome's favor.

[276] I.e., Bocchus and Sulla.

[277] The Balearic Islands (in the eastern Mediterranean) were colonized by the Phoenicians in remote antiquity. They had a reputation for proficiency with the sling. *See* Strabo III.5.1; Livy XXXVIII.29.

[278] The Paeligni were a Italic tribe who inhabited the region now known as Abruzzo.

himself ready, checked his arms and weapons, and activated all his senses; there was some fear, but a greater amount of confidence, as naturally adheres to the victors when facing those whom they have often defeated. Meanwhile the cavalry scouts sent to conduct reconnaissance reported that nothing appeared hostile, as was indeed the case.

CVI. Volux approached the quaestor and addressed him, saying that he had been sent by his father Bocchus to intercept them and act as armed guards. They linked together that day and the following one without any trepidation arising. After this—when the camp had been constructed and it was evening—the Moor, terrified and with his face contorted, ran to Sulla and told him his patrols had learned that Jugurtha was not far away; Volux at the same time urged and implored Sulla to escape with him secretly during the night. But with a defiant spirit Sulla denied that he was afraid of the Numidian whom he had defeated so many times; he had enough faith in the martial virtue of his men. Even if certain destruction was at hand, he said, he would rather stand firm than abandon the men he was leading, thus saving by ignominious flight an uncertain life destined to end soon, perhaps, through illness anyway. When Volux advised that they should set out during the night,[279] Sulla agreed to the plan; he ordered the men to eat their evening meal immediately, to build as many camp fires as possible, and to slip away in silence at the first watch.

When all the men were exhausted from the forced march at night, Sulla at first light was measuring the dimensions for a camp. Moorish cavalry scouts suddenly announced that Jugurtha had taken up a position about two miles in front of them. After learning this, our men were gripped by momentous fear: they were convinced they had been double-crossed by Volux and were now trapped in an ambush. There were some who said he should be

---

[279] Meaning to set out as a whole force, not to escape as individuals.

executed, and that he should not be permitted to evade the consequences of such a treacherous act.

CVII. Sulla ordered his men not to do the Moor any injury, although he thought the same as they did. He exhorted the soldiers to maintain a strong fighting spirit: there were many previous examples in history of a small, disciplined number fighting successfully against a sizeable enemy. The less they worried about their own safety in battle, he said, the safer they would be; neither was it right for any armed man to look to his unarmed feet for assistance, or to turn the blind and exposed part of his body towards the enemy at a time of supreme fear. After invoking the great Jupiter as witness to Bocchus's criminality and treachery, Sulla then ordered Volux to be expelled from the camp, since he had proven himself to be an enemy. Weeping before the Roman, he begged Sulla not to believe his suspicions: what had happened was not due to perfidy but to the cleverness of Jugurtha, who almost certainly had learned of their journey from his network of informers.

Because Jugurtha did not have a large number of men, Volux claimed, and was hanging all his hopes and resources on Bocchus, he believed the Numidian king would not dare to do anything while his son[280] was there as a witness. For this reason, the best thing to do would be to cross openly through Jugurtha's camp; Volux said he himself would go alone with Sulla whether the Moorish troops were sent ahead or left there. This plan seemed well-advised considering the situation. They set out immediately; and because their scheme took the enemy by surprise, they moved through untouched while Jugurtha wavered in doubt about how to respond. A few days later they eventually reached their intended objective.

CVIII. There was a Numidian there named Aspar who happened to be a close associate of Bocchus. He had been sent by

---

[280] Volux.

Jugurtha (once the king had heard that Bocchus requested to meet Sulla) to eavesdrop on Bocchus's plans and to act as his secret informer. There was also a man named Dabar, the son of Massugrada, who came from the clan of Masinissa; he was of lowly origins on his mother's side—as her father was the child of a concubine—yet very dear to, and valued by, the Moor because of his many good character traits. Bocchus's experience had been that Dabar had shown loyalty to the Romans many times previously, so he sent him without delay to Sulla to announce that he was prepared to do whatever the Roman people wanted.

He proposed that Sulla should designate a day, place, and time for a dialogue, and that he should not be afraid of Jugurtha's ambassador. He was preserving good relations with Jugurtha, he said, so that their common interests could be more easily handled.[281] It would not have been possible to protect himself against Jugurtha's schemes in any other way. More than the stated reason, though, I think it was more due to Punic faith[282] that Bocchus misled both the Romans and the Numidian with the hope of peace. Alone with his thoughts, he debated at length whether to turn over Jugurtha to the Romans or Sulla to Jugurtha: his deepest desires weighed against us, but his fears argued for us.

CIX. Sulla then indicated that he would say a few words in front of Aspar; as for the other communications, the speaking would have to be done either secretly[283] or with as few others present as possible. At the same time Sulla told his envoys how they should answer. After the conference had been scheduled as

---

[281] Meaning the common interests between Bocchus and Sulla. Sallust is saying that Bocchus wanted to keep his relations with Jugurtha in a "holding pattern" until he had a chance to meet secretly with Sulla. Bocchus is scheming to betray his former ally and does not want to arouse Jugurtha's formidable suspicions.

[282] "Punic faith" was a famous Roman pejorative term for treachery.

[283] I.e., the other communications would have to be done in secret with Bocchus.

he had wanted, he said he had been sent by the consul to ask whether Bocchus wanted peace or war. Then the king—as he had already planned on saying—ordered him to come back in ten days; he had not, he claimed, made any decision yet, but would disclose it on the appointed day. Each of them then returned to their respective camps. Yet when a good part of the night had gone by, Sulla was secretly summoned by Bocchus; both of them were accompanied by interpreters of proven reliability, with Dabar—a man held in the highest esteem by both sides—also present to help mediate the proceedings. The king then began in this way.

CX. "I never thought the time would come when I—the greatest sovereign in this part of the world and of all the kings I know—would owe thanks to a private citizen. By Hercules, before I knew you there were many who petitioned me for help; I provided hope to some men on my own, since I required nothing from others for myself. I myself was happy to carry this heavy burden, although some are accustomed to be distressed by it. To feel a sense of need: this for me will be the measure of the price paid for your friendship, for nothing is more dear to my heart.[284] As verification you ought to consider this: feel free to take arms, men, money, and finally whatever your heart desires. Make use of them, and as long as you live, you should never think you have any reciprocal obligation to me. For me it will always be considered settled. If I am aware of any need of yours, you will finally want nothing from me in vain. As I see things, it is less humiliating for a king to be defeated in war than to be exceeded in generosity.

"Please accept a few words from me about your republic, as whose ambassador you have here been sent. By no means did I

---

[284] By accepting Sulla's "friendship" (a courteous way of saying that he now agrees to become a Roman vassal) he will have to give up his freedom of action. Independence is traded for security, an idea fundamental to the expansion of all empires.

make war on the Roman people, nor did I want this to happen; I have safeguarded my frontiers with arms against armed incursions. I will stop doing this, since it displeases you: continue with war with Jugurtha as you wish. As for me, I will neither go beyond the Muluccha river nor permit Jugurtha to cross it, as it was the border between myself and Micipsa. If you seek anything else appropriate between the two of us, you will not leave here unhappy."

CXI. Sulla replied briefly and courteously to these sentiments, invoking the necessity of a peaceful settlement and their shared interests. Yet he revealed to the king that the senate and Roman people would feel no reassurance in his verbal guarantees, since the Romans had bested him on the battlefield. Some positive act must be done that would clearly be in the Romans' favor instead of his own; such an opportunity was readily available since he had access to Jugurtha's forces. If he turned Jugurtha over to the Romans, he said, they would be very much in Bocchus's debt; at that point, he would certainly have Roman friendship, a security pact, and that part of Numidia that he coveted.

The king at first was unwilling to do this; he claimed that his familiarity with Jugurtha, their shared bonds, and their mutual treaty rendered this impossible. Beyond this, he worried that such a display of disloyalty would incite the minds of the common people for whom Jugurtha was a cherished figure and the Romans a focus of hate. Eventually a fatigued Bocchus was softened by Roman persistence, and in the end he promised to do everything that Sulla wanted. As an additional matter they concluded a simulated peace that the Numidian, fed up with war, had ardently wanted. The scheme having been agreed on, each side then withdrew.

CXII. The next day the king sent for Aspar, Jugurtha's representative, and told him that he had learned from Sulla (through Dabar) that it was possible to conclude an armistice; he should, for this reason, probe his king's thoughts on the matter.

Aspar at once made his way to Jugurtha's camp. Having been given full guidance on what to do, he rushed back to Bocchus eight days later and announced to him that Jugurtha would be able to do everything Bocchus wanted, but that he had little confidence in Marius. Many times before, he said, peace had been concluded with Roman generals to no avail. Furthermore, if Bocchus was talking to both parties and wanted a conclusive peace, he should at some point schedule a meeting under the guise of a peace conference and there turn Sulla over to him. He was convinced that once he had such a public figure as a hostage, a treaty would then come by order of the senate or the people; a man of noble birth would not be left in enemy custody when he had gotten there not because of his ineptitude, but while honorably serving the state.

CXIII. Turning these considerations over in his mind, the Moor finally extended his promise.[285] We have insufficient information to determine whether his reluctance was genuine or due to cunning; but it often happens that the motives of kings, despite being ardent, are fluid and on occasion at cross-purposes to each other. Later when the time and place for the peace conference were designated, Bocchus spoke both to Sulla and to Jugurtha's representative; he received them both with royal niceties, extending the same guarantees to both of them. Both were equally impressed and filled with positive expectations.

But that very night—which was the one before the day set for the conference—the Moor gathered his confidants together and at that very moment changed course by switching out old plans with new ones. He is said to have carried on a fierce inner conflict with himself, with his eyes and face as turbulent as his heart; although he was outwardly silent, these volatilities revealed the hidden sentiments of his heart. Eventually he ordered Sulla to be brought

---

[285] I.e., he promised Jugurtha he would do what he asked.

before him; and in accordance with the Roman's wishes, he prepared for the betrayal of the Numidian. When daylight came and he was told that Jugurtha was not too far away, he formally proceeded with a few attendants (as if he were intending to pay his respects to Jugurtha) and our quaestor[286] to a small hill that was within easy view for those who were lying in wait. As had previously been agreed, the Numidian also came unarmed with a few of his attendants; a signal was then given, and then immediately from every side he was swarmed by concealed enemies. Jugurtha's attendants were cut down; he was shackled and delivered to Sulla; and from there he was led before Marius.

CXIV. At the same time our generals Quintus Caepio and Cnaeus Manlius were utterly shattered by the Gauls.[287] All of Italy shook with fear at this news. At that time and even down to our own living memory the Romans subscribed to the idea that every other military task was a simple matter for their martial virtue, but that with the Gauls they fought not for glory but for survival. But when it was announced that the war in Numidia had come to an end and that Jugurtha was to be brought to Rome in chains, Marius (who was not present)[288] was appointed consul and the province of Gaul was delegated to him. On the Kalends of January[289] the consul celebrated a triumph in a halo of glory. And at that time the hopes and resources of the nation were placed on him.

---

[286] *Quaestore nostro*, meaning Sulla.

[287] A reference to the Battle of Arausio on October 6, 105 B.C. The Cimbri and the Teutoni routed the Roman armies whose losses may even have exceeded those at the Battle of Cannae against Hannibal.

[288] He was elected *in absentia*. This was rare. Marius would eventually hold the office of consul an unprecedented seven times in his career.

[289] January 1st.

XI. Translator's Postscript

So Sallust ends his narrative of the Jugurthine War. The ultimate fate of the Numidian king was a grim one. According to Plutarch (*Life of Marius* 12), he and his two sons were led in chains before Marius's chariot in a triumph in Rome. He was by this time a shell of a man; Plutarch relates that Jugurtha's defeat and humiliation had precipitated a complete nervous breakdown. After enduring the scorn and jeers of the crowds gathered to see the spectacle, he was then led to the Tullian prison, the same dungeon where the Catilinian conspirators had met their own ends. As Jugurtha was lowered into the hole, he is reported to have said, "By Hercules, what cold baths you have!" Plutarch wrote that he survived for six more days before dying. The historian Eutropius, writing in the fourth century A.D., claims that Jugurtha was strangled by order of the consul.[290]

As the personalities of Marius and Metellus occupy a central position in *The War of Jugurtha*, it will be useful to relate more information about them here. Caius Marius (157 B.C.—86 B.C.) was a complex and driven man who defies easy classification. His positive contributions to the Roman state were considerable: he reformed the organizational structure of the Roman army, changed the military recruitment system, brilliantly defended Italy against invading Germanic tribes, and held the consulship an unprecedented seven times. He rose from modest origins to become for a time the most powerful man of the republic. But at

---

[290] *Breviarium* IV.27.

the same time he was jealous, vindictive, conniving, and unrelentingly ambitious; and these character flaws would prove to be his undoing. Sallust duly notes Marius's constant undermining of his military superior Metellus while in the field in Numidia. Indeed, Marius never misses an opportunity to spread malicious rumors about his boss: such disloyalty among military men in wartime is unforgivable and he was lucky to have escaped severe punishment for it. Never satisfied with his victories, Marius would go on to battle other ruthless generals like Sulla for control of the Roman state. His fortunes fluctuated considerably; but in the end he emerged victorious, entered Rome in triumph, and died of natural causes while serving his seventh consulship.

Sallust's opinion of Marius was pragmatic and somewhat detached: he recognizes the general's unsavory character traits but gives him his due as an influential figure in Rome's development. A corroborating opinion was held by the historian Velleius Paterculus (who was also a military man). Writing around 30 A.D., Velleius describes Marius as

> A man of rural origins, uncultivated and coarse, rigid in his personality, as great a general in times of war as he was pernicious in times of peace; he was a man of unbridled ambition, insatiable, always unrestrained and restless.[291]

These words have the ring of truth. Velleius also takes note of Marius's maneuvering to replace his superior in Numidia at a time when the war against Jugurtha had already been, as he says, "essentially won."[292] Yet his influence on Roman history was considerable and lasting. If we measure greatness by historical

---

[291] *Historiae Romanae* II.11. The original words are *natus agresti loco, hirtus atque horridus vitaque sanctus, quantum bello optimus, tantum pace pessimus, immodicus gloriae, insatiabilis, impotens semperque inquietus.*
[292] Id.

influence, there can be no doubt that he was a great man. Yet few would call him a good man. Plutarch notes that he became so vengeful after his final return to power that, like the dictators of our own time, he would unhesitatingly put men to death if they displeased him. His ambition allowed him no rest; Plutarch's description of him in his final years is anything but positive. It is a portrait of an empty, lonely soul, a man for whom even absolute power was an inadequate salve for his agonies:

> But Marius himself was now an exhausted man. He was, as it were, afloat on a sea of anxieties and utterly tired out. It was too much for him to have to think once more of yet another war, and to imagine new struggles, fears which he knew from experience to be well-founded, and the weariness of it all...Above all things he feared the sleepless nights and so he indulged in heavy bouts of drinking at all hours of the day and in a manner most unsuitable to his age, trying to induce sleep as a refuge from his own thoughts.[293]

Plutarch presents Marius as a man who, despite all his military victories and mastery over others, never found the courage to master his own insatiable cravings and omnipresent fears. He contrasts the pathetic image of Marius in old age with the simplicity and wisdom of the Greek sages who found contentment in lives of simplicity and honor:

> There is...the case of Antipater of Tarsus who, they say, when he was in the same way [as Marius] near death, counted up all the blessings of his life and did not even forget to mention the good weather he had had on his voyage

---

[293] *Life of Marius* 45. *See* Warner, Rex, *Plutarch: Fall of the Roman Republic*, London: The Penguin Group (2005), p. 54.

out of Athens, thus showing how deeply grateful he was to a benevolent fortune for every one of her gifts, and how he had laid them up safely in that most secure of human treasure-houses, the memory, to the very end. Thoughtless and forgetful people, on the other hand, let everything that happens to them slip away as time passes. And so, laying hold of and retaining nothing, real good always eludes them; instead they fill themselves with hopes, and neglect the present while they fix their eyes on the future. Yet what happens in the future is subject to fortune, whereas the present cannot be taken away…For dealing with the blessings which come to us from outside we need a firm foundation based on reason and education; without this foundation, people keep on seeking these blessings and heaping them up but can never satisfy the insatiable appetites of their souls.[294]

The life of Metellus was much different; in many ways he was Marius's polar opposite. Quintus Caecilius Metellus (c.160 B.C.—91 B.C.) was a conservative aristocrat as well as an educated and cultured man. Velleius Paterculus describes him as a man "second to no one of his era."[295] He studied philosophy in Athens before entering a military and political career; after his recall from Numidia he was surprised to find a grateful reception waiting for him in Rome. In recognition of his services in Africa he was awarded the cognomen Numidicus. After the conclusion of the Jugurthine War, he was elected censor and became a prominent voice in the conservative faction opposing the populist Marius; the two men would never reconcile. After losing the complicated political struggles that followed, he agreed to a

---

[294] Id., p. 55.
[295] *Hist. Rom.* II.11.

voluntary exile in order to spare the state extended civil strife. Accompanied by a scholar, he left Rome and traveled to the island of Rhodes to continue the philosophical studies that had been such a consolation to him in his youth. He did not surrender himself to despair; in time he would return to Italy and died in Rome in 91 B.C. He was a good man, as well as a great one.

INDEX

www.ingramcontent.com/pod-product-compliance
Lightning Source LLC
Chambersburg PA
CBHW021827090426
42811CB00032B/2051/J